20 TRUTHS
THAT HELPED ME IN MY BATTLE WITH
PORN ADDICTION

A 40-Day Study Journal

STEVE GALLAGHER

20 TRUTHS

THAT HELPED ME IN MY BATTLE WITH

PORN ADDICTION

A 40-Day Study Journal

For books and other teaching resources please contact:

Pure Life Ministries
14 School Street
Dry Ridge, KY 41035
(888) PURELIFE - to order
www.purelifeministries.org

20 Truths that Helped Me in My Battle with Porn Addiction
Copyright © 2024 by Pure Life Ministries.

ISBN/EAN 979-8-218-38301-5

A Special Note of Thanks

Like most books, this study journal is a result of someone having a vision for it. My name is on the cover, and indeed, I did write the Bible studies for each day's homework. But it was Patrick Hudson, the Ministry Outreach Coordinator at Pure Life Ministries, who had the vision for this study guide. He also played a key role in the development of much of the content.

I also wish to acknowledge the contributions of other members of the Pure Life Ministries team: Pastor Ed Buch, who reviewed and edited all of the content; Pastor Nate Danser, who worked with numerous members of our counseling department to develop the Reflection Questions; Jonathan Willetts, who created the cover and interior designs; and all those Pure Life graduates who contributed their inspiring stories of how God rescued them and gave them a new life in Him.

Contents

INTRODUCTION

If you are addicted to pornography, your sexual lusts probably seem like a mountain standing before you. No doubt, in the past you have attempted to scale that mountain many times, only to get part way up and then experience a failure and slide right back down—more discouraged than ever.

To get free from a porn addiction, one must scale the mountain and then live the rest of his life on the other side of that mountain. But the key to accomplishing this feat is actually counterintuitive. You must forget the mountain altogether. The problem with staying focused on scaling that summit is that it keeps your attention off of the true source of lasting victory.

Rather than constantly focusing on that mountain, I propose that you set it aside and develop a new lifestyle. That new way of doing life is what will take you over that peak and keep you on the other side. Once a new way of living is established in you, even if you do experience setbacks along the way, they won't be so devastating that you will throw up your hands and give up.

Allow me to share a story with you that occurred a number of years ago. A young man named Charles[1] had entered the Pure Life Ministries Residential Program. He came to us from a past of drug addiction and habitual homosexual activity. He later wrote about what happened during his first days at Pure Life Ministries.

---

1   A pseudonym.

Because I only went there to deal with "my issues" (which centered only around my struggles with homosexuality), humbling myself to others or even being merciful to an undeserving individual were concepts foreign to me and of no great interest to me. However, as I began to read "At the Altar of Sexual Idolatry," I was exposed. I got my first glimpse of how corrupt I was and how ignorant I was of the true character and nature of God—despite the fact that I professed that I loved God. Nevertheless, I found hope... there was a way out that I did not quite understand yet.

One of the early problems Charles had was that he felt we weren't spending enough time addressing his "issue," i.e., homosexuality. He had arrived at Pure Life Ministries with a stack of books describing in great detail all the problems associated with the "gay lifestyle." He thought our entire focus would be on his same-sex attractions so he was very disappointed to see how little we talked about those issues.

I told him, "Charles, I understand that homosexuality is a mountain in your life; its shadow looms largely over everything else. But for the next nine months, I want you to *set that mountain aside and make knowing the Lord the primary focus of your life.*" And that's what he did.

So nine months later I had another conversation with him. I asked him, "Charles, you have really pressed in to know the Lord during your time in the program. Now tell me, where is the mountain?"

"That mountain is gone," he assured me.

Yes, he overcame his addictive behavior, not because he made the victory his great goal, but because he made knowing the Victor the subject of his attention.

Having shared that story with you, I want to say the same to you: If you will go after the Lord in a meaningful way, you are going to achieve the victory you desire. But don't get all hung up on how you're doing. Just keep pressing into the Lord and watch Him do what only He can do.

Let's Get Started

Perhaps you have already watched the series this study journal is based on: *20 Truths that Helped Me in My Battle with Porn Addiction*. The fact is that each video is jam-packed with important information you need, but the problem is that it comes at you too quickly! So the purpose of this study journal is to help you slow this process down a little and dig deeper into some of the vital truths that I shared in the videos—truths that I learned through my own battle out of sexual addiction and also those I've garnered through nearly 40 years of intense counseling with countless other porn addicts.

What you have before you is a 40-day journey that should take you where you want to go: into freedom! Here's how we've set up this journal. Each of the twenty videos in this series has two days of Bible study assignments for you to complete that are tied to it. The way it is designed is for you to first watch the video for that day and then do the related assignments. (It wouldn't hurt to watch the video again before completing the second day's assignments as well.)

After you've watched the video, you'll read a testimony from a graduate of the Pure Life Ministries Residential Program. These men have been where you are now, with their own seemingly insurmountable mountain in front of them. But all of them took their eyes off that mountain and found lasting victory through a new, deeper life in Christ. It's our hope that their stories will encourage you. Trust me, if God can do it for them, then He can do it for you too.

The rest of the assignment for that day will include a Bible study on a topic from the video, followed by reflection questions to help you apply that topic to your own life. Learning what Scripture has to say and allowing it to examine and alter your own life are vital to developing the new lifestyle you need.

Once you've completed the homework assignment, you might even want to dig deeper in Scripture by doing your own supplemental Bible study on that particular subject. The more you invest in this, the greater your encounter with the Lord will be, and the more you will get out of this journey. If you will work through this study journal the way it is intended, you will see yourself making real progress in overcoming your sin.

Look, I'm not going to sugarcoat this. You have dug yourself into a pit that isn't easy to emerge from. Nevertheless, I have seen countless men get the victory over habitual sexual sin and there is no reason you can't gain that freedom as well.

So why not get started right now?

Getting Started:

Each day's video is available at purelifeministries.org/20-truths or by scanning the qr code in the chapter header.

Scan to download an editable PDF if you prefer to take notes digitally:

Day One

HOPE

Watch Truth #1:
There is a Way Out

Carter's Story (Graduated 2021)

In spite of the fact that I grew up in a decent Christian home, I got involved in pornography at an early age. This didn't stop me from becoming deeply involved in church activities. In fact, I eventually attended Bible college with the idea of pursuing ministry.

During my time there, my long-lasting struggle with pornography grew worse. I became so heavily controlled by it that I ran up a great deal of debt, not caring about the financial consequences I was incurring. It was all part of my instantaneous lifestyle that eliminated any ability to think about the future. To me, the future would just be more of the same hopeless misery I was experiencing then.

My sexual sin got so bad that I started using dating apps to hook up with women. By the time I graduated from college, I was completely lost, utterly given over to sexual sin and committed to its ways. Any thought of getting free seemed hopelessly distant and far away.

Eventually my secret life came into the light and I was confronted by my spiritual leaders. They presented me with an opportunity to pursue the Residential Program at Pure Life Ministries. I agreed to go, but I was so far gone that I wasn't even sure I wanted to be free.

Nevertheless, the Lord met me where I was at and helped me to start facing the reality of who I was and what I had become.

He also started teaching me to repent. I learned that God could transform my heart if I would begin humbling myself. This was a challenge to me because in the past I was so manipulative with others that I wouldn't acknowledge being wrong about anything. But as I began humbling myself, He really did start that work of transformation in my heart. In fact, He actually gave me the capacity to care about others in a real way. Through this process my need for the Lord's grace every day has become very real to me.

My life today is vastly different from where it was just a few years ago. The Lord has redeemed a lot of things in my life such as friendship, ministry and my outlook on the future. Yes, there are still times of strong temptation and maybe even failure, but when I am faced with strong temptation, I now know how to fight. Yes, sexual sin once dominated my life, but I've begun to taste the true life that comes through Jesus Christ.

A Study in God's Word

Like Carter's story, there was a time when the main driving force of my life was lust. It kept me going from week to week—always looking for my next sexual exploit. My life really was a miserable existence of always feeling dissatisfied—nothing ever scratched the relentless itch that drove me on. Eventually it all came crashing down. But there in the heap of ashes that had been my life was a tiny flower called hope. I hadn't felt it in years. It was just enough to get me headed back in the right direction.

> ✍ **Write out and then memorize Hebrews 11:1.**

01   Explain in your own words the role hope plays in a believer's faith.

02 Carefully consider the following verses which contain the word hope. Explain what point you think the author was making in each verse.

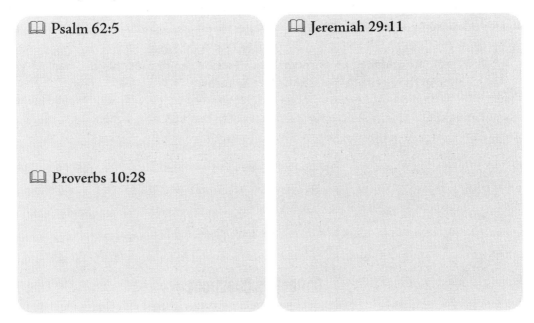

📖 Psalm 62:5

📖 Jeremiah 29:11

📖 Proverbs 10:28

The standard of living in America far exceeds any people group that has ever lived. Of course, it isn't our fault that we live in such a wealthy nation, but that doesn't alleviate our responsibility to limit its effects on our spiritual life. Prosperity has a way of subtly leading Christians into a mindset of self-trust. If we can get by in life through our own efforts, why would we feel a need to rely on God?

03 Look up 1 Timothy 6:17-19 and explain the point that Paul was making.

Another inescapable result of prosperity is indulgence, and unrestrained indulgence inevitably leads to addiction. I suppose there is nothing that can more effectively quench a person's hope for the future than to be addicted to some vice that demands one's entire devotion.

04   If you are addicted to pornography, describe the impact this has had on your hope in the Lord and your hope for the future.

Reflection Questions

Before I got into my testimony in the video, *There is a Way Out*, I shared my desire that you would come away with the attitude, "If that guy can get free, anyone can!" Did my story leave you with the firm conviction that you can have a life that isn't dominated by sexual sin? Take a few minutes to think deeply on this.

01   How would the spiritual quality of your life (relationship with God and others, outlook on the future, ability to be productive in school or career) improve if sexual sin was behind you forever?

02 What things have you already tried in an effort to break free from pornography or other habitual sexual sins?

03 Has the fact that you've tried other things that haven't produced a life of victory left you wondering if the Lord is even able to deliver you?

🕊 **Prayer Point**
Read 1 Corinthians 10:13, 1 Corinthians 15:17, and Psalm 107:10-16. If you have had difficulty believing that God has the power or willingness to bring you into freedom, spend some time before Him confessing the sin of unbelief. Then, ask Him to renew your faith in His character and power.

Day Complete ✓

Day Two

LIVING IN THE MIRACULOUS

Dylan's Story (Graduated 2016)

I grew up going to church and living a profession of faith that appeared to be real to those around me. However, behind all the smiles, church attendance and mission trips was a secret life of sin I had kept hidden from everyone for over fifteen years. Looking back on that time now, I can see that there was no power in my life to really live for God. I was basically living the Christian life "in the flesh."

In 2015, I spent five months in Brazil as part of a mission team. I restrained my pursuit of illicit sexual pleasure while I was there, but when I returned to my former job in downtown Nashville, my double lifestyle reemerged. I went right back to drinking, doing drugs, and having random hookups in secret.

Although this bondage continued, I was unwilling to admit it to anyone else. I even maintained that I knew the Lord, in spite of the fact that there was no power of God over sin in my life. I would often tell myself, "I know I will eventually outgrow this issue—especially if I get married." I was blind to the depth of my sin and the effects it was having on my relationships with those around me. Every step into sin was taking me further into an ever-greater deception.

In the meantime, I had applied online to go on another mission trip. During the application process, the counselor wrote me that everything looked good, but he wanted to revisit one of the questions that was lacking detailed information. The question was regarding the history of my sexual sin.

As I read his email it was as if everything came to a halt. I was confronted with the reality of where I was and where I was heading. It was not an audible voice, but I knew in my heart Almighty God was speaking very clearly to me. I could either continue lying about who I was—and even go on this mission trip—or I could come into the light by telling the truth. There was no getting away from the choice sitting in front of me. Never in my life had I encountered the presence of God in this way. I was in great trepidation as I deliberated between the two alternatives. As I considered the ramifications of this decision, I realized that it was going to cost me everything if I chose to confess my hidden sin. My life would never be the same again.

This experience served as the catalyst to get me to Pure Life Ministries. The Lord met me there powerfully and gave me the grace to come into the light about my sin for the first time. The conviction of the Holy Spirit led me into true repentance and a supernatural regeneration of my heart. God gave me new birth and put His Spirit in me. After that, the miraculous work of Almighty God continued as He persistently and lovingly drew me to Himself.

Looking back I see God's divine work of taking my unresponsive heart and giving me a new one. Now I know the supernatural power of God through faith in Jesus Christ, no longer by mere profession, but by the life He now lives in me and through me.

A Study in God's Word

I want to begin today's study by touching on a very precious possession of yours. I'm referring to your Bible. That book is the historical narrative of God's miraculous interactions with mankind during the first 4,000 years of this earth. When God is at work in people's lives, supernatural things occur.

01   Look up the following verses and briefly describe what God did that was out of the ordinary of human life as we know it.

📖 Genesis 5:24

📖 Genesis 15:1

📖 Genesis 7:17

📖 Genesis 19:24

📖 Genesis 11:9

📖 Genesis 19:26

📖 Genesis 12:17

📖 Genesis 20:18

📖 Genesis 21:2

We haven't even made it half-way through the first book of the Bible and God has already performed at least nine miracles—some of them nearly unfathomable. And miracles continue as part of God's work among men all the way through the Old Testament. He parted the Red Sea for the children of Israel and brought down the walls of Jericho. Through the power of Yahweh, Daniel survived the lion's den and Elijah called down fire from heaven.

Now, fast forward to First Century Judaism and suddenly the miracles are nonexistent. Formal religion has taken the place of the supernatural. The Pharisees knew the Scriptures and were exceedingly religious. Yet they were blind to the fact that the Son of God was in their midst.

02   Can you see how religious activities can take the place of possessing the life of God and the miraculous living that should accompany it? Explain the difference you see between a religious lifestyle and a life that is controlled by the Holy Spirit.

Now, fast forward again, this time into 21st Century American Christianity. Once again we find a religious system that largely lacks the miraculous. I believe that much of this is due to a lack of true supernatural conversions.

It seems that most Christians have grown up in church and learned how to "become" Christians by adapting into their lives the unspoken rules of conduct inherent in the denominational culture they are a part of. One might even call this "Christian atheism." What I mean is that there are many professing Christians who mentally ascribe to the tenants of the faith, faithfully attend church services every week, yet lack the kind of supernatural activity one would expect to find in the life of a person who is indwelt by the Spirit of God. Their "faith" in God doesn't seem to reach into their hearts.

03   Read the story of Jesus returning to His hometown in Matthew 13:53-58 and explain in your own words the dynamic at work in the people of Nazareth and then compare it to the lack of the miraculous at work in the lives of American Christians.

Reflection Questions

01   Take a few minutes to think back on your own Christian history. Describe some of the more notable incidents you have experienced that can only be regarded as something beyond the scope of the explainable—something supernatural. If you haven't experienced anything you would consider to be beyond the scope of natural life, just say that.

02 Based on what you've learned today, would you say that your life has been characterized by a living and miraculous relationship with God, or has it been characterized by religion that lacks the power of God?

03 I think it's fairly obvious to assert that those who walk closely with God will have a greater experience of His power in their lives. What are some areas of your life that would need to change in order to have a closer relationship with God? (Focus your list on other things beside sexual sin struggles).

Whether or not you have experienced the supernatural activity of God, one thing is certain: if you are addicted to pornography, you need God to perform a miracle in your life. To be gripped by a habit—to commit the same sinful activity time and time again with an inability to stop—means that your only hope is for God to do the needed work inside you to set you free.

Believe me when I tell you that He wants you to walk in victory. The truth is that He wants you for Himself and this idol of sex is keeping you from Him.

🕊 **Prayer Point**
This might be a good time to pour your heart out to the Lord, asking Him to do for you what you cannot do for yourself.

Day Complete ✓

Day Three

DECEPTION

Watch Truth #2:
Sexual Sin is a Liar

Chase's Story (Graduated 2021)

My teenage years were a time of experimenting with many different kinds of drugs and getting involved with a number of short-term girlfriends. By the time I was nineteen, my life had gotten so out of control that I entered a fourteen-month residential program for drug and alcohol abuse. I met the Lord there at some level and was able to overcome my drug and alcohol habits.

After I graduated from the program, I was invited to join their staff. Within a year I was appointed to be the instructor of their curriculum to the twenty-plus students in the program. This meant that I had a lot of spiritual authority and influence over their lives.

I talked to the students a lot about having a life of freedom, but I always kept these discussions limited to freedom from drug abuse. What I didn't talk about was the fact that I was becoming increasingly addicted to pornography and sexual sin. My desire to portray a godly image to my family and to the ministry leaders was far more important to me than actually living a godly life.

I did pretty well at keeping my sexual sin hidden from others, but my lack of true godliness would come out in various ways. For example, I would cover students' sin from the other leaders if I thought it would get them in trouble. I even proudly confessed my own secret sin to a few guys that I knew would be impressed that I was hooking up with women. The shallow kind of Christianity I portrayed taught them that it was okay to teach the Bible while engaging in hidden sin as long you didn't cross some imaginary line of wickedness you had come up with in your own mind.

Eventually I moved on from that organization and started my own outreach ministry through the medium of Christian Hip-Hop. I would share my testimony of being set free from drugs and alcohol in churches and drug rehabs throughout the country. During this entire time I deceived myself into thinking that doing some outwardly good deeds would actually cover the most heinous of sins. I really believed that I was walking with the Lord. Because of my delusion and low standard of Christian living, I also continually deceived those around me into believing that they too could live carnally and still be pleasing to the Lord.

A Study in God's Word

✏ Write out and then memorize Hebrews 3:13.

One of the many biblical terms used to describe deception is the Greek word *apatao* (and its strengthened form, *exapatao*). This term is usually used in the sense of *masking the truth with the purpose of enticing a person into sin*. This sense is very clearly seen in the Septuagint (Greek Old Testament) version of the story of Samson and Delilah. The Philistine leaders offer Delilah 1,100 pieces of silver if she would deceive Samson into telling her the secrets of his power. Their instructions? "Entice (*apate*) him, and see where his great strength lies…" (Judges 16:5)

01   Using what you learned from the italicized definition in the above paragraph, look up and rewrite the following verses in your own words—without using the words "deceit" or "deception." Don't worry about saying it exactly right; this is just an exercise to get you to really think through these verses. The first one is completed for you as an example:

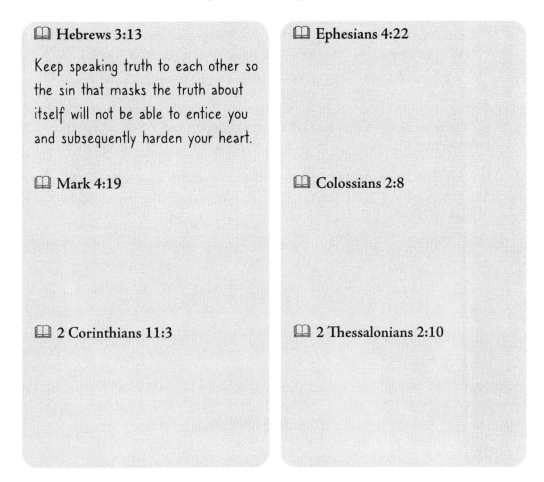

📖 Hebrews 3:13

Keep speaking truth to each other so the sin that masks the truth about itself will not be able to entice you and subsequently harden your heart.

📖 Mark 4:19

📖 2 Corinthians 11:3

📖 Ephesians 4:22

📖 Colossians 2:8

📖 2 Thessalonians 2:10

Take a look at the kinds of things which deceive us (sin, riches, the enemy, your old self, false teachers and the antichrist) mentioned above. Delilah could be considered a personification of sexual sin and the way it deceives those who indulge in it.

02 Can you see how pornography has lied to you? Explain your answer.

03 Consider the following statements and, using your own words, sum them up into a comprehensive paragraph that reflects what you have learned.

"Nothing can deceive unless it bears a plausible resemblance to reality."
C.S. Lewis[i]

"You've got to deceive yourself before you can be deceived."
Anonymous[ii]

"People are only vulnerable to being deceived when they want what is being offered to them."
Steve Gallagher[iii]

Reflection Questions

01 As you've learned in today's study, sin is a master deceiver. Sin masks its true nature, promising to benefit us in some way, but in the end always bringing pain and suffering into our lives.

A   What benefits did you hope you would gain by pursuing sexual sin? Be specific.

B Have you found that sexual sin has ever delivered on its promises?

C What destructive things have been introduced to your
   life because of your involvement with sexual sin?

D Are you still believing the lie that sexual sin will
   be a benefit to you in the future?

In the video, I mentioned five lies that Christians in sexual sin believe. Our prayer is that God will use this study journal to instill the necessary truths into you that will bring you into lasting freedom.

02 Read the following list of lies. Pick two that you have believed in the past and explain how believing that lie has hindered you from gaining the victory over sexual sin.

A Sexual sin will always be an awesome experience.
B There will be no lasting consequences when I sin.
C I am a godly guy with a little sin problem.
D My sexual sin isn't that bad.
E Other people are the cause of my problems.

Day Complete ✓

Day Four

SEXUAL SINNERS TEND TO BE LIARS AS WELL

Nicholas' Story (Graduated 2022)

I guess the best way to describe my life before coming to Pure Life Ministries would be that I was a man who was living two separate lives.

Those around me would have characterized me as a "good guy." I was seen as being warm and compassionate; hardworking and successful; someone who was committed to God and loved his wife; a God-fearing family man who loved to sing exuberant praise to the Lord during church services.

They saw this side of me because that's what I constantly portrayed to others. In fact, I was so good at presenting this image that I actually came to believe it about myself.

The truth was that I had a very ugly side that very few ever saw, which included committing adultery at every opportunity. I would try to make up for this by buying my wife flowers and treating her with kindness. How shallow and worthless all of that seemed to her when she discovered the truth about what I was doing.

This double life of sin and hypocrisy nearly drove me insane. A deep-seated anxiety about my secret life being exposed relentlessly gnawed at me. I lived with the constant fear of losing the respect of my wife and others. Instead of leading to honesty and repentance, this fear only drove me to try harder at enhancing my "good guy" image.

I honestly feared that if someone found out about my sin they would label me "a dirty sex addict." In spite of my behavior, I convinced myself that "that wasn't the real me." I refused to admit to myself that I actually was a sex addict. I thought "yeah, I have a sin problem," but I tried to make up for it through my persona of being a good guy.

The more I built up this image, the more I believed I *was* the image and not the ugly thing underneath. "After all," I would tell myself, "I'm doing all these good things. I may give into adultery every once in a while, but the real me is the one that wants to be good."

I actually believed that I loved my God, my wife and even the women I seduced into sin. The truth was that there was only one person I really loved: ME. I *wanted* to love myself and I wanted everyone else to love me as well. I wanted my wife to see me as an amazing husband. I wanted other women to want me because I was a sensitive and fun lover. I wanted to be adored by my Church because I was always involved in Christian activities. I wanted to be favored by God because I was such a good Christian.

I was in such delusion about where I really was that if someone questioned my behavior, I would try to make them feel guilty for daring to think less of me than the amazing image of myself that I was projecting.

It actually wouldn't be until I had a genuine encounter with the Lord at the cross that I came into the reality of who I truly was. The truth I discovered there began the undoing of my fake persona and the start of a real life in Jesus Christ.

A Study in God's Word

Professing Christians who are engaged in sexual sin nearly always hide from others what they are doing in secret. It is the double life that goes hand-in-hand with addictive behavior. But what is at the root of this deception? I addressed this in my book, *Walking in Truth in a World of Lies.*

01   After reading the following quote, explain in your own words how this dual-sided motivator played a part in maintaining your double life.

Why do people act as though they are living at a certain spiritual level when they clearly are not? The motivating factor of hypocrisy really boils down to the two-sided motivation of wanting to receive the approval of others and/or fearing their disapproval. If a person acts in such a way that he "loses face," he knows he will be treated with little respect. On the other hand, if he acts in such a way that he gains the approval of others, he will be praised. The human ego constantly strives to avoid losing face and to gain [admiration].[i]

✍ Write out and then memorize Mark 7:6.

02 Look up the following statements. Take some time to ponder and meditate on what Jesus said about hypocrisy and write a paragraph in your own words that sums up the various things He taught about it.

📖 Matthew 6:2

📖 Matthew 6:5

📖 Matthew 6:16

📖 Matthew 23:25

📖 Matthew 7:5

📖 Matthew 23:28

📖 Matthew 23:23

03 Read Proverbs 28:13 in your personal Bible and then compare it to the following paraphrased translations. After you consider these complementary variations, explain in your own words the point Solomon was making in this statement.

"He who keeps his sins secret will not do well; but one who is open about them, and gives them up, will get mercy."
Bible in Basic English

"You will never succeed in life if you try to hide your sins. Confess them and give them up; then God will show mercy to you."
Good News Bible

"Never shall you thrive by keeping sin hidden; confess it and leave it, if you would find pardon."
Knox Bible

Reflection Questions

01 If someone was able to see both the image you project of yourself and the way you live your life when no one is watching, what disparities would they see?

1 John 1:9 is the "go-to" verse in the Church for people dealing with addictive behavior. However, it has been my experience that most people have a fairly shallow perspective on the spiritual truth John was communicating. Biblical confession involves two functions: (1) an admission of guilt, and (2) a thorough acknowledgement of the wrongness of it.

02 Consider how you have handled your involvement in pornography. Explain any confessions you have made about it and how they line up with the two functions of biblical confession listed above.

Day Complete ✓

Day Five
SIN CORRUPTS

Watch Truth #3:
*Sexual Sin Comes
With a Price*

Zach's Story (Graduated 2015)

When sexual sin began to take over my life, it was only one piece of a larger puzzle—the life of selfishness I had constructed over the years. That selfishness functioned like a cancer that gradually eroded my character. Although I was blessed that my parents paid my tuition for college and graduate school, this afforded me a lot of free time. Unfortunately, I wasted much of it on worthless pursuits such as endless hours surfing the internet and watching movies. All of this came at the expense of my studies and what could have been worthwhile friendships.

Needless to say, this lifestyle quickly led me into pornography. My sex and entertainment-driven life spiraled out of control, eventually crossing lines I never imagined I would cross. Within ten years of getting involved with porn, I was living in open homosexuality.

After years of this self-indulgent living, my mind and heart were so eroded that I could hardly function as a person. The career as a professional musician that I had pursued was in a shambles after losing one job after another. For years afterward, I had recurring nightmares of running late to a concert and walking onstage after the performance had already started… which wasn't too far from the truth!

By the time I arrived at Pure Life, I was in a daze, full of spiritual darkness and worn out by my unrestrained lifestyle. This left me continually plagued by a sense of condemnation and alienation from God. I hardly remember anything my counselor said to me in those early days, because I would come into my sessions barely able to think straight!

One of the first things I needed to do was to start chipping away at the lazy, self-centered lifestyle I had developed. This meant starting to focus my mind and heart on the Lord and other people. Little by little this brought about greater inward stability and peace.

I still go through struggles in my thought life, but they don't consume me like they once did. The quickest way for me to get out of the downward spiral of temptation is to shift my thinking off of myself and start focusing on the Lord and other people. It is amazing how quickly this shifts my momentum and gets me out of any spiritual darkness developing in my heart. My former life was a path into the darkness, but now, "the path of the righteous is like the light of dawn that shines brighter and brighter until the full day." (Proverbs 4:18)

A Study in God's Word

Over the course of the next two days, I want to touch on a couple of the inevitable consequences of habitual sin. Both were mentioned in the video, but I think it would be worthwhile to take a deeper dive into these two side-effects of illicit behavior.

Let's begin with what happens to the inward life. In the video I used Paul's statement that "the wages of sin is death" to help explain how sin corrupts a person. But the Bible also uses the agricultural metaphor of sowing and reaping to describe the inevitable results of sinful actions. Seed is sown into the ground and grows up into a full plant which eventually yields fruit. The idea of sin leading to death is much the same, but the agricultural metaphor better illustrates how corruption is worked into us over time.

01 Read the following verses and explain in your own words what each one adds to your understanding of this principle.

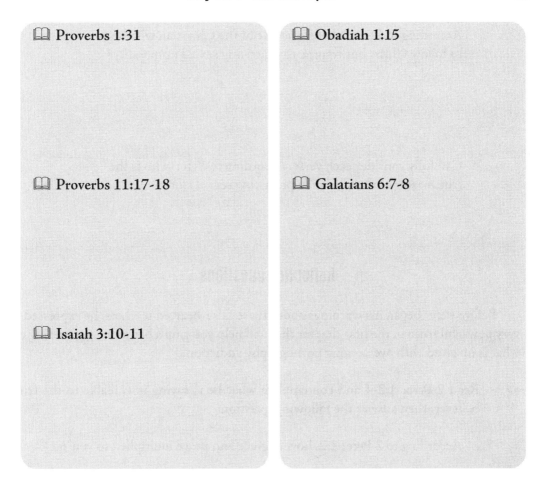

📖 Proverbs 1:31

📖 Obadiah 1:15

📖 Proverbs 11:17-18

📖 Galatians 6:7-8

📖 Isaiah 3:10-11

Each of these passages uses the metaphor of sowing and reaping, but it is the passage in Galatians that hits on the soul corruption that follows sin. The Greek term is *phthora*, which literally means to decay or ruin. It is sometimes translated with the word "corruption," and sometimes with the word "destruction."

02 Another passage that describes the spiritual fallout that comes with habitual sin is 2 Peter 2:18-22. Read through the passage and answer the following questions:

A Although this passage is primarily talking about false teachers, the issue is not what they teach, but about how they are living their lives.

According to Peter, what is the fate of the Christian who begins to follow Christ but returns to practicing sexual immorality?

B Carefully consider each verse. According to Peter, who is the true master of the Christian practicing sexual sin?

Reflection Questions

Before Peter began his warnings about these false-hearted teachers, he expressed a very powerful truth in the first chapter that will help you gain a better understanding of what is involved with overcoming pornography addiction.

01 Read 2 Peter 1:2-4 and contemplate what he is saying is available to the true believer; then answer the following questions.

A According to 2 Peter 1:2, how is "grace and peace multiplied to you"?

B According to 2 Peter 1:3, what is it that "has granted to us everything pertaining to life and godliness?" Explain what that means.

C The second phrase of 2 Peter 1:3 reinforces the important role an intimate relationship with the Lord plays in the life of a believer. To "know the Lord" means more than possessing information about Him; it means to know Him by having a personal, intimate relationship with Him as a person. Explain where you are in this lifelong process.

D According to 2 Peter 1:4 believers have been granted "His precious and magnificent promises." Write out three biblical promises that you can think of pertaining to God's aid in your spiritual growth.

1

2

3

E According to the next phrase in 2 Peter 1:4, those promises will help you "become partakers of the divine nature." Describe in your own words what that means.

F The last clause in 2 Peter 1:4 describes something believers must do for the different aspects of this spiritual process to kick in. Explain in your own words what "having escaped the corruption that is in the world by lust" means.

02 Considering all that you have studied today, explain the important role your relationship with God plays in finding freedom from the corruption of sin in your life.

🕊 **Prayer Point**
Doing this 40-Day Study Journal should be helping you learn how to sow to the Spirit. Take some time right now to ask the Lord to help you apply the truths you've learned so far. If you lack a strong desire to live a righteous life, don't despair, just take that need to the Lord. That is a prayer He is sure to answer!

Day Complete ✓

Day Six

THE IMPORTANCE OF THE HUMAN CONSCIENCE

Luis' Story (Graduated 2019)

I was first introduced to sexually explicit material when I was seven years old. Rather than telling my parents about that accidental discovery, I allowed its tantalizing effects to take root in my heart. This undoubtedly played a part in me developing a physical relationship with a neighbor girl that continued into our teenage years. In the meantime I discovered online pornography, which quickly escalated into years of addictive behavior. Throughout middle school and high school, I never denied myself the pleasure of fantasy, pornography or masturbation. By the time I entered Bible school, I was using drugs and alcohol and engaging in sexual relationships with various girlfriends.

All of this served to harden my heart and sear my conscience. I attempted to escape the relentless guilt I was experiencing by playing videogames at every opportunity. This only offered temporary relief, though. So I decided I needed to fill my life with upright activity. For instance, I became class president and became heavily involved in my church. Looking back I can see that I was trying to overcome my sense of guilt through a misguided attempt to win God's favor through my own righteousness. But nothing I tried alleviated those nagging feelings of guilt and shame.

I eventually ended up at Pure Life Ministries, but in spite of the fact that I attempted to deal with my problems in my own way, God didn't deal with me harshly or condemn me. Instead, He met me in a very sweet and lowly way. It was His love and humility that won me over. What drew me to Him was how night after night He allowed me to *experience* His love even though I had been such a wretched sinner. There were nights I would lay in the snowy fields looking up at the stars, filled with awe at how little I was in light of God. This further softened my heart toward Him.

I am now free from habitual sexual sin and no longer take advantage of others. When I do violate one of God's laws in some way, I no longer run from the feelings of guilt and pain. I let the Lord deal with me. The blood of Jesus and His righteousness washes my conscience clean. I'm no longer fearful of facing my guilt because I see His incredible love for me. I now desire to serve Him and honor Him, and I know those things would be impossible without a tender and clean conscience.

A Study in God's Word

One of God's greatest gifts to mankind is the conscience. In the video I said, "God gave man a conscience as an inward monitor of the rightness and wrongness of his actions." The conscience plays a vital role in the life of a believer, and yet it can be damaged to the point of losing its ability to function. I can think of three influences that can damage it.

The first occurs when social conscience goes awry. We live in a time when good is called evil and evil is called good. The more we allow that godless mindset to blare its message into our heart, the more it can diminish our own sense of right and wrong. Before long, evil doesn't seem quite as bad and goodness doesn't seem quite as good as they once did. This is another reason believers should limit the influence the world has on their hearts.

The second phenomenon that has greatly diminished the social morals within the evangelical community is the overall effect that humanistic psychology has had on Christians. In his typical straight-forward style, John MacArthur shares his impression of this belief system.

> *The goal of modern psychology is to train people to ignore their conscience. Your conscience is making you feel guilty? That's wrong. You're not a bad person, you're good, you lack self-esteem. In fact, you're so much better than you think you are that it's really troublesome and most of your problems are because you don't know*

how good you really are. So when conscience says you're guilty, you're guilty, this is wrong… It's very important that you not believe the psychological lies today of those who want to dispossess you of any guilt and make you feel completely exonerated from any guilt of any kind. That is a very, very devastating way to silence a God-given warning system in the souls of men and women.[i]

Both of these influences can affect the conscience's ability to perform its tasks. Perhaps you can see how the culture you have grown up in or the humanistic thinking of our time has dulled the way you view sin, including sexual sin. This does not excuse you of your guilt, but explains why it can be so easy to fall victim to pornography's lure. However, neither of these influences can deaden a person's conscience like the actual indulgence in wicked behavior. While the first two can influence you to give over to wickedness and vice, sinful activities themselves will begin to distort your thinking, dull your emotions, and corrupt your very soul.

01   Read Romans 2:15 and describe in your own words how "the Law" (i.e., the Word of God) affects a person's thinking.

02   Read 2 Corinthians 1:12 and describe how Paul's clean conscience provided him with a sense of assurance in his walk with God.

In his first epistle to Timothy, Paul exhorts him to "fight the good fight, keeping faith and a good conscience, which some have rejected and suffered shipwreck in regard to their faith." (1 Timothy 1:18-19) Paul is making a connection between fighting the good fight of faith and the state of one's conscience.

03   Explain this connection in your own words and the outcome of one's life who would reject that fight.

04   Look up 1 Timothy 4:1-2 where Paul returns to the subject of the conscience and explain in your own words what he is warning end time believers to watch for.

05   In his letter to Titus, Paul once again addresses the conscience. Read Titus 1:15 and explain in your own words the spiritual reality he is describing.

Reflection Questions

01 Earlier I mentioned how our culture and humanistic psychology can both have a
negative effect on people's consciences. Write a paragraph explaining how these
influences may have impacted your own life and conscience.

02 Identify five ways that pornography and other forms of ungodly entertainment have deadened your conscience and killed your desire for godly things.

A

B

C

D

E

☑ **Action Step**

Considering what you have learned about the important role your conscience plays in your walk with God, describe what you must do for it return to its original healthy condition. Also write out any steps you can take to begin implementing those things into your life.

Day Complete ✓

Day Seven
GOING ASTRAY

Watch Truth #4:
*Go Near the Prostitute's House
and You Will Get Burnt*

Blake's Story (Graduated 2007)

Shortly after becoming a Christian at the age of thirteen, I stumbled onto the path of sexual sin that would dominate my life for the next decade.

It happened one day when I was mindlessly wandering through TV channels. Suddenly, there it was: my first glimpse of sexual sin. I became riveted by what I saw on the screen. Instead of running in the opposite direction, I stopped dead in my tracks with that proverbial "deer in the headlights" look. Having been raised in church, I instinctively knew this was something forbidden. But I liked it. And I wanted more of it.

With that scene emblazoned on my mind, my eyes were on the prowl, constantly looking for sexuality anywhere I might find it. The internet hadn't yet become embedded in the culture at that point, so my sources for lascivious fare were TV, movies, billboards, magazine racks, and pretty schoolmates. Having conditioned my mind in this way, once the World Wide Web was at my fingertips, it didn't take me long to find hardcore pornography. It was as if porn was waiting for me. Once I discovered it, I devoted all my energy to pursuing it.

I could not stop thinking about porn. My life became a relentless search for its fleeting pleasures. Even though it always left me filled with guilt and shame, it took only the slightest provocation to inflame my lust. Over the years, I became increasingly more determined to find it, spending thousands of dollars on it in the process.

But even as my sin intensified, so did my attempts to get free from it. Accountability groups, counseling, and many, many books—but all were powerless to curb the monster within. It was during this time of great struggle that I met the love of my life. I honestly believed that getting married would bring this nightmare to an end, but it wasn't long before I was right back into it again. Living with my wife just created a new obstacle to get around.

She eventually discovered my secret life and separated from me. I knew then that I needed to do whatever it took to find freedom. As I did a web search, urgently needing an answer, Pure Life Ministries showed up.

It was in the Residential Program, that my mind began to shift from centering on sexual things to dwelling on the Lord. It was this constant focus on Him that persuaded me to begin taking the necessary steps back toward my heavenly Father. In all my years of seeking porn, He was always waiting for me, His prodigal son, to turn back to Him. My hopelessness brought me to an end of myself and opened my eyes to the pig pen I had been in. It was there at the cross that I really found the Lord.

Having been reconciled to God through Christ, I have found true satisfaction and pleasure. Porn's seductive voice only offered momentary gratification, yet always ended in despair and misery. I have found a better lover. Greater than that, the true Lover of my soul found me and gave me a life that I never thought was possible. All those old avenues of sin no longer appeal to me, and I'm all the more careful about what I put in front of my eyes. Those days of careless drifting are over because I've found my rest in the Lord.

A Study in God's Word

In the video I took a look at Solomon's description of sexual temptation in Proverbs chapter 7. Take some time to read that passage before starting today's devotional. You may even want to substitute the word "pornography" wherever you see the word "prostitute."

The concept of falling away from one's walk with God is reflected in various terms in Scripture. To waver, backslide, wander away, turn aside, go astray and commit apostasy are a few terms used in the Bible. Two of these words show up in Proverbs 7:24-27.

These terms would certainly apply to a professing Christian who allows himself to become sucked into the dark and evil realm of pornography. Surely the final verse should be enough to make any porn addict shudder: "Her house is the way to hell, descending to the chambers of death." (Proverbs 7:27 NKJV)

So today we'll examine the two Hebraic terms Solomon employed in verse 25 of this passage.

> 💾 **Reread and memorize Proverbs 7:25 in your own translation.**

The first word in the Hebrew that we'll consider is *satah*, translated in the NASB as "turn aside." This choice of words sounds rather innocuous until the Hebrew term is examined more closely.

Take, for example, the remarkable test for adultery contained in the Torah. If a wife is accused of having "gone astray" (*satah*) "into uncleanness," (Numbers 5:19), a priest would administer an otherwise harmless concoction of water and barley to the woman. If she was innocent, nothing would come of it, but it was another matter if she was guilty.

01   Look up Numbers 5:27 and describe the outcome if she had, in fact, committed adultery.

02   What does this outcome reveal about how God views sexual sin?

The second term we'll look at is *ta'ah*, translated in Proverbs 7:25 as "stray." Here again to "stray" seems pretty innocuous—like a guy walking down a road who, through no fault of his own, is somehow diverted into a ditch. Here again we need to take a closer look at how this word is used elsewhere. The most famous verse utilizing this verb is Isaiah 53:6—"All of us like sheep have gone astray, each of us has turned to his own way..."

03 Consider the following verses supplied below where *ta'ah* is underlined. Write a short paragraph describing what you learn about this term and explain how it could be used to describe the effect sexual sin has had on your life.

"But they did not listen, and Manasseh <u>seduced</u> them to do evil more than the nations whom the LORD destroyed before the sons of Israel."
2 Kings 21:9

"For forty years I loathed that generation, and said they are a people who <u>err</u> in their heart, and they do not know My ways."
Psalm 95:10

"The wicked have laid a snare for me, yet I have not <u>gone astray</u> from Your precepts."
Psalm 119:110

"He is on the path of life who heeds instruction, but he who ignores reproof <u>goes astray</u>."
Proverbs 10:17

"The righteous is a guide to his neighbor, but the way of the wicked <u>leads</u> them <u>astray</u>."
Proverbs 12:26

"Will they not <u>go astray</u> who devise evil? But kindness and truth will be to those who devise good."
Proverbs 14:22

Reflection Questions

01 In Proverbs 7:6-10, a young man wanders at twilight down a road that will take him near a prostitute's house. When he gets in the vicinity, she comes out to seduce him. Does this story have any parallels with your life when you were first introduced to pornography? How so?

02 In Proverbs 7:11-20, Solomon describes how the prostitute acts toward this young man. She is bold and alluring. She is daring and tells him that no one will ever know what they will do in secret. I'm sure you can see a clear parallel between the prostitute's lies and those told you by pornography. Why do you think we believe the lies of sexual sin?

03   In Proverbs 7:21-23, Solomon shows the result of this young man's folly. From your own experience of being lured into the same trap, what kind of advice would you give your younger self? What kind of wisdom would you impart to someone else?

Prayer Point

Now take some time to meditate on the advice you just wrote down, and ask the Holy Spirit to help you apply this wisdom to your own situation when facing sexual temptations.

Day Complete ✓

Day Eight

KEEPING

Liam's Story (Graduated 2020)

Before I started putting time into reading God's Word, I had no desire or power to resist the temptation to sin. If the desire and opportunity were present, I quickly surrendered to the temptation. However, when I began reading the Word, the Lord used it to put a fire in me to resist sin and surrender to Him instead.

I grew up in a Christian home, did all the Christian stuff, and had a good image both inside and outside the church. However, during my teenage years, I began to spend a lot of time on my computer, drinking in the online culture. This led to a slow, but steady, slide into sexual sin. It began with occasionally looking at images; then progressed to seeking out videos on seemingly innocuous sites like YouTube; then to openly seeking sin on websites devoted to it. Ultimately, I ended up involved in sexual relationships. Without the Word, I had no sense of my need to live a godly life and no desire to change. I thought I was a good guy who wanted to do the right thing and that ultimately things would just "work out."

When I began reading the Word, I was confused by what I read. I had grown up with a nominal, contemporary American view of Christianity; I believed the right stuff, confessed Jesus as Lord – that was it, right? But the Word showed me I did not love God and was not living as a disciple of Christ. This shook me to the core and instilled in me a desperation for true life. As I continued to read the Word, the conviction of sin grew so strong inside me that I became tormented about my spiritual condition. I knew I could not allow sexual sin to persist in my life.

One day, after giving over yet again, an overwhelming frustration with myself and hatred for my sin welled up within me, and I knew I could never go back to it. I suddenly realized I had the ability to say "no" the moment a thought entered my head and move my mind away from it. I had never had this power before. It had hardly even occurred to me to try to fight, much less believe that I could win the battle. But the Word had changed my thinking. The Lord taught me to "take every thought captive" (2 Corinthians 10:5 ESV), without my even having to consciously apply the verse.

Since that day, the Lord has kept me from going back to my sin as I have continued to submit my will to His and to what He has revealed to me in His Word. Each day is a battle, and I must choose to resist temptation moment by moment. But the Lord has given me the Holy Spirit to enable me to walk out that which He has called me to, and He has given me the power to say "no" to sin. It's not rules or fences that keep me; it's His Word and the work He has done inside me by the power of the Holy Spirit.

A Study in God's Word

✍ Write out Proverbs 7:1-2, 5 from your favorite translation.

Most translations of Proverbs 7:1-2 use the word "keep" (Heb. *shamar*) in both verses. According to Strong's Concordance, the Hebrew word *shamar* means "to hedge about; i.e., to guard." This term is of great importance for those who are being tempted by pornography, because it shows us that our spiritual lives are not solely God's responsibility—He expects us to do something!

01   Look at the following uses of the word *shamar* and describe in your own words what you learn about the believer's responsibility regarding his spiritual life.

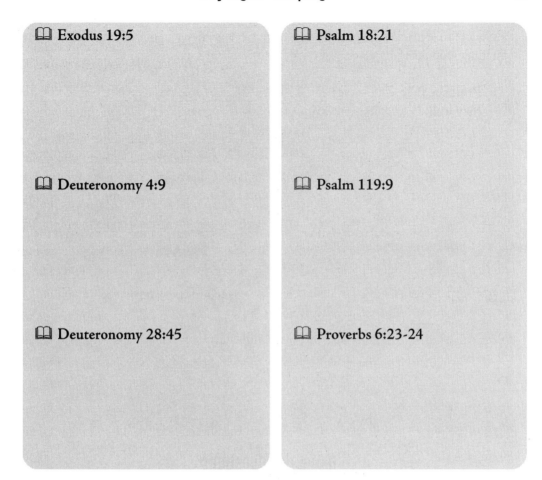

📖 Exodus 19:5

📖 Deuteronomy 4:9

📖 Deuteronomy 28:45

📖 Psalm 18:21

📖 Psalm 119:9

📖 Proverbs 6:23-24

02 Re-read Proverbs 7:1-2. In light of what you've learned about *shamar*, write a short paragraph about the importance of keeping God's Word.

Now read Proverbs 7:3-5. What we see here is that when we keep God's Word, something wonderful happens: God's Word then keeps us.

03   Read the following verses and describe what people can expect from God when they walk in obedience to Him.

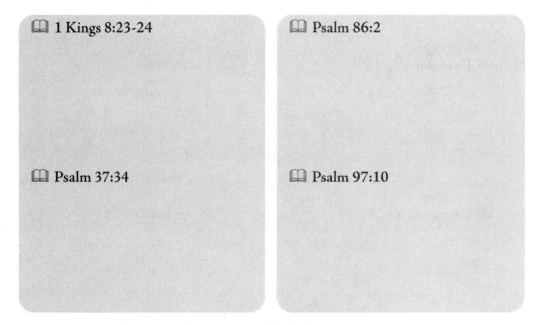

📖 1 Kings 8:23-24

📖 Psalm 86:2

📖 Psalm 37:34

📖 Psalm 97:10

Reflection Questions

01   Both Psalm 119:67 and Proverbs 6:23-24 show us that God often uses difficulty in order to help us learn to obey Him and keep His Word. What current circumstances in your life might God be trying to use as "affliction" or "discipline"? What lessons might God be trying to show you through these circumstances?

02 Have you experienced times when God intervened to keep you from sinning? What does this show you about His power and His character?

03 Considering all you've learned today regarding the importance of keeping God's Word, spend some time reflecting on how you are doing in that area. Then, write down several specific ways you see your need to change or improve.

I'm sure you realize that temptations can arise at very unexpected times. This is why the video stated that the three main things a man can do to keep his mind and heart are to, "ask the Lord for strength to endure, spend time in the Word, and focus one's thoughts on the things of God."

☑ **Action Step**

As preparation for today's temptations, write Psalm 119:9 on a notecard and meditate on it throughout the day. And remember, if God has mercifully stepped in at times to keep you from committing the sins you wanted to, how much more will you experience His keeping power when you are really walking with Him?

Day Complete ✓

Day Nine

A PICTURE OF INSANITY

Watch Truth #5:
*Sexual Addiction is the
Epitome of Insanity*

Rich's Story (Graduated 2006)

Insanity! Yes, that was me and how I lived my life! Every day I would spend hours looking at porn and indulging my sexual lusts, all the while seeming to be a decent guy to those around me.

The scary thing about it was my utter delusion. In spite of the fact that I was living in my own little world of sexual fantasy and erotic filth, I came to believe myself to be the nice guy I portrayed to others. I had given over to the lusts of my heart for so long that I actually thought the evil desires within me were a manifestation of love for others.

By this point, I had pretty much lost all sense of right and wrong when it came to issues of morality. All I cared about was

indulging my lust. In fact, my whole life revolved around it. I cared little for anyone or anything else; my only concern was how I could gratify my insatiable desire for more. Gone were the pangs of conscience and the guilt associated with my sinful behavior. God was distant. I was walled off from friends and loved ones. Eventually I became paranoid, full of fear that others would find out about my shameful life of secret sin. I was so terrified of ruining my reputation that I couldn't bring myself to confess to anyone about my addiction to sex.

Whenever anyone would confront me about something—no matter how trivial it might be—I always had an excuse. As far as I was concerned, I was never wrong about anything. I blamed everything and everyone but myself. One time my mother challenged me about my selfishness and I yelled at her saying, "I am not selfish—how dare you say that I am selfish!" She was absolutely right, but because of my tirade, she later repented for what she had said, even though I was the one who should have been repenting to her!

Yet, God didn't give up on me and eventually began to bring me to my senses. My conscience revived to the point that I knew I could no longer continue in my sinful behavior. The extreme guilt and shame was more than I could bear. Somehow, in a moment of clarity I knew that my sin was not okay and that I needed to find freedom at any cost!

Finally, in His mercy, God gave me the courage to confess my hidden sin to my pastor. Around this time, I also heard about Pure Life Ministries and their Residential Program. I continued to seek freedom on my own but to no avail. Eventually I enrolled in the program at Pure Life and I have never looked back. God has set me free and continues to keep me free!

A Study in God's Word

Many years ago I wrote a magazine commentary entitled, "God, can I plead insanity on Judgment Day?" The title was an allusion to the American court system which does not hold a person responsible for their actions if they have been deemed "insane." The point I was making in the article was that there is an increasing unwillingness in our culture (and even in the Church) to accept responsibility for one's actions. But, however people may justify their behavior, they will be held accountable for the things they have done on Judgment Day.

People are not born insane. They end up in that frightful condition through a long series of choices. In other words, such people established a pattern of thinking and acting with complete disregard of God's rule of law. Solomon brought out this reality when he wrote, "…the hearts of the sons of men are full of evil and insanity is in their hearts throughout their lives." (Ecclesiastes 9:3) I guess you could say that every human heart has insanity in it—the level being determined by the amount of sin one has indulged.

I can think of no greater example of this in Scripture than that of King Saul. He began his reign as king of Israel by courageously mustering Jewish men to defeat the Ammonites who were terrorizing the Israelites of Jabesh-Gilead. He seemed the perfect choice to lead the nation, but he eventually proved himself utterly unfit for such a high calling. His final downfall began when he was given a clear command by the Lord through Samuel the prophet.

01 Read the story of Saul's rebellion in 1 Samuel 15 and answer the following questions.

A According to v. 3, what did God tell Saul to do?

B Read v. 9 and explain how Saul only partially obeyed God's command.

C According to v. 11, what was God's attitude about his partial obedience?

D According to v. 13, how did Saul present his actions?

E Read 1 Samuel 15:14-21 and describe in your own words the various ways Saul attempted to minimize his disobedience.

F Read 1 Samuel 15:22-23 and explain in your own words what you think Samuel meant by what he told Saul.

G In v. 24, Saul seemed to acknowledge his sin. Explain how he attempted to justify himself.

H   According to v. 26, what was Samuel's final verdict regarding Saul?

02   At the beginning of this day's study the assertion was made that people only become insane when they establish a long pattern of defying the commands of God. In 1 Samuel 18:10, we see the final outcome of Saul's pattern of disobedience. Read that passage and write down what you observe.

Reflection Questions

Hopefully you've realized from today's study that when people choose to think and act in a way that defies God's laws, He eventually will remove His restraining grace from their lives, leaving them incredibly vulnerable to the forces of evil. In extreme cases, this could be a raving lunatic in a secure hospital ward; but more typical would be everyday people who are tormented by fears, paranoia, depression, lust, anger, etc.

01   As you think about this list, are there particular ways you are tormented or plagued with various mental struggles?

02   Feelings of guilt inevitably follow sinful behaviors. One of the most common ways men respond to this guilt is to minimize how sinful their actions really are. What are some of the ways that you have attempted to minimize the sinfulness of your pornography use, or any other sexual activities you have indulged in?

03   As Saul increasingly walked in disobedience, he was plagued with various torments. Do you see a connection between what you're now experiencing and disobeying God's command to abstain from sexual immorality? How so?

In the video, you heard the statement that one characteristic of an insane person is extreme self-centeredness. And the horrible reality about pornography is that this is the very attitude that it fosters.

04   Think about your life. In what other ways does self-centeredness manifest in your actions? In your interactions with others? In your attitude?

Read Romans 12:1-2 in your favorite translation.

Here it is in the Phillips translation:

With eyes wide open to the mercies of God, I beg you, my brothers, as an act of intelligent worship, to give him your bodies, as a living sacrifice, consecrated to him and acceptable by him. Don't let the world around you squeeze you into its own mould, but let God re-mould your minds from within, so that you may prove in practice that the plan of God for you is good, meets all his demands and moves towards the goal of true maturity.

05 What encouragement does this passage offer you in this journey of transformation?

Day Ten

IDOLATRY

Logan's Story (Graduated 2016)

"Hear, my son, your father's instruction, and forsake not your mother's teaching," (Proverbs 1:8 ESV) My father warned me many times about the dangers of viewing pornography and my mother would plead with me in tears to turn from my ways, but against all wise counsel, I chose to pursue my sinful desires. While I knew what I was doing was wrong, I had no idea the extent of the damage my sinful choices would cause, nor the price it would cost me.

My parents' instructions were not the only commands I disobeyed. I had read the Bible and grew up immersed in a Christian environment. So I knew Scripture clearly states that sexual immorality is sinful and that it has serious consequences. But despite all of these warnings, I was determined to find my pleasure in sexual promiscuity.

An idol can be described as anything we are willing to sin to obtain. I know this from experience because I lived in sexual idolatry for nearly two decades. What started off as a porn addiction developed into a lifestyle of frequenting massage parlors and hiring prostitutes. Underlying my sinful behavior was a high-minded attitude of self-importance.

My entrance into the dark world of pornography destroyed my ability to comprehend the spiritual danger I was in. It's as if my mind was being taken over by a foul spirit that presented each image or video as a new object for me to worship.

Eventually my mind became so perverted with fantasy that I began to lose all sense of reality. Everything was viewed through the lens of sex. And after multiple failed relationships and countless hours and dollars wasted on sin, I finally hit rock bottom and entered the Residential Program of Pure Life Ministries.

God was longsuffering with me. In His mercy and compassion, the Lord helped me to see that my sinful behavior was the product of idolatry. I responded to His conviction by taking full responsibility for my sin and sincerely repenting of it. I asked the Lord to break me of my obsession with sex and to help me fix my eyes on Jesus.

Through a daily walk of repentance, I have been able to develop a lifestyle of true worship to God alone. There are times I can be tempted to take my eyes off Him, but by living in the light and holding myself accountable, the Lord has kept me free from the lifestyle of idolatry that once consumed me.

A Study in God's Word

In Satan's long war against God, sex has arguably been his most effective weapon against those who wish to follow God. Other than Solomon's warnings in the book of Proverbs, sex isn't overtly mentioned a lot in the Old Testament (OT). In fact, the words "sex," "fornication," and "homosexuality" are not mentioned a single time. Nevertheless, it was a problem of immense proportions throughout the history of Israel.

From the very beginning Satan has sought the worship of humans. In ancient times he accomplished this through idolatry, which is mentioned some 600 times in the OT. The main draw to these ancient fertility cults was sex with female (and often male) temple prostitutes.

One of the earliest stories of idol worship is found in Numbers 25 where Midianite women were sent into the camp of the Israelites when Balaam advised "Balak to put a stumbling block before the sons of Israel, to eat things sacrificed to idols and to commit acts of immorality." (Revelation 2:14) Once the Israelites entered Canaan, idolatry gradually supplanted the worship of Yahweh until, at long last, He was forced to send them into captivity. It was there that the love of idolatry with all of its sensuality was purged from the Jewish nation.

01   Read the first two of the Ten Commandments found in Exodus 20:3-5.

A   What reason did the Lord give in v. 5 for issuing these two commandments?

B   Explain why you think He listed these two
    commandments before the other eight.

02 Read Exodus 34:12-16 and explain in your own words what you learn.

Both idolatry and sexual sin can draw a man away from a submissive life to God. Rather than making God's commandments and values the basis for how he lives, a satanic mindset begins to dictate his beliefs. The rebellious lifestyle of one indulging in habitual sexual sin is outright treason to the laws of God's Kingdom.

03 Proverbs 5 is one of those OT passages that tackles sexual sin head on. Read
    that chapter and explain the point he was making in your own words.

04 The apostle Paul provided two lists of the kinds of activities people are engaged in who "will not inherit the kingdom of God."

A   What are the first four practices listed in Galatians 5:19-21?

B   What are the first five practices listed in 1 Corinthians 6:9-10?

Reflection Questions

In my experience, those who are addicted to pornography are usually willing to see sexual sin as an idol. What they often miss is that they also have a host of other idols they have placed above God.

01 List three activities in your life that you place more importance on than spending time in the Word of God.

A

B

C

Prayer Point
Spend some time asking the Lord to reveal to you the reason why you pursued these activities so passionately.

02 What did the Lord reveal to you? What did you hope those activities would give you?

A

B

C

☑ **Action Step**
What is one thing you could begin doing every day that would put Jesus into a more prominent place in your heart and life?

Day Complete ✓

☑ FIRST CHECK-IN

At this point in your journey, some changes in your life should be taking place. I'm not necessarily saying that you are walking in complete freedom from your addiction to pornography, but you should definitely be making some progress.

Don't despair if you feel like you haven't changed a bit. That is very typical. The important thing at this point is to see your *inner attitudes* beginning to change. The desire to become free should be growing within you. The belief that you can actually be free from pornography should be becoming more real to you. You've only just begun this journey. Remember: God's desire is to deliver you and set you free! Keep turning your heart to Him and crying out to Him for the power and endurance you need.

Now, here are some practical commitments that will be key in your own battle against pornography.

☐ **I will do this study every day.**

> One of the things you will learn later on in this study journal is that overcoming something as powerful as pornography requires a daily habit of spending quality time with the Lord in Bible study and prayer. If you will commit to doing this study every day, that habit will be established by the time you finish this study journal!

☐ I will cut off all avenues to pornography.

If you're in the early days of fighting your way out of addiction, you need to put barriers between yourself and pornography. Temptation can strike at any moment, and you haven't yet developed the self-control to resist the powerful pull of porn. By cutting off every open avenue to pornography (installing an internet filter, locking down your smartphone, deleting any downloaded porn videos, etc.), you will make it much more difficult to fall into sin (which is a really good thing!). Identify your vulnerabilities and get protected right away!

☐ I will open up to my spiritual leader about my secret life.

Sin thrives in the dark, but it dies in the light. Maybe you've never told anyone about your secret life, or maybe you've made some vague confessions here and there. That has to change if you want real freedom. It's time to really come clean with the truth about how you've been living. Contact someone you can trust (a pastor or mature believer) and tell them that you need to confess some sin. When you meet with them, give them the full picture of what you've been doing. It may be one of the hardest things you've ever done, but by bringing your sin into the light you will make massive strides toward real freedom.

🕊 Prayer Point

How about spending a few minutes before the Lord, consecrating yourself and establishing these commitments? Ask Him for the help you will need for the long haul.

Day Eleven

THE PLACE OF PLEASURE

Watch Truth #6:
Behind Sexual Addiction Lies the Pleasure Hormone

Wyatt's Story (Graduated 2015)

When I was a kid, having fun meant everything to me. Some would say that's normal, that kids are supposed to have fun. And that's true; but I took that attitude with me into adulthood.

My childhood was fairly sheltered, so my pleasures were innocent for the most part, like reading and playing educational games on the family computer. Even though these could rightly be considered "good" activities, they began to take such a place in my life that I had no patience for doing anything I didn't want to be doing. Any task I was given would always take much longer than it should have because when no one was looking I would abandon the task and find something I wanted to do.

I'm sure this all seems pretty innocuous, right? However, this pattern of life set the stage for the discovery of pornography in my middle school years. I had so engrained the habit of giving into my every whim that I had no strength or even desire to resist. I knew it was wrong and would tell myself "I'm never doing that again," only to find myself going right back to it.

My desire for pleasure only increased when I went away to college. It was there that I discovered the vast variety of entertainment available on the internet. I quickly lost any restraints I had, spending hours watching movies, binging on television series, and playing video games—hours that should have been spent studying. I had to pull several all-nighters writing papers because I had completely ignored the assignment until the night before it was due. I knew that I *should* be getting started on that paper, but always wound up doing what I *wanted* to be doing instead. I had no strength to say "no" to my desire for pleasure. I just did not have the wherewithal to discipline myself to do life's most basic tasks.

Of course, this lifestyle of pursuing the pleasure found in entertainment fed my addiction to pornography as well. I was so used to giving in to the desire for entertainment that, even though I knew pornography was wrong, I couldn't quit giving over to it. Instead, I would spend hours wandering across the internet, searching out anything that came to mind.

It took seven months in the Residential Program—away from all the games, worldly movies, and distractions of the internet—for my addiction to entertainment to be broken. The Lord showed me how much my love for pleasure had been feeding my addiction to pornography. I came to realize that if I was going to walk with Him, I must be disciplined in every area of my life. It is not always easy. For instance, maintaining a consistent daily devotional life has been one of the biggest challenges I have faced after the program. However, every day He gives me the strength and will to deny my flesh and to pursue a life with Him.

A Study in God's Word

Making pleasure the most important aspect of one's life could be compared to a teenager who thinks he can live on candy bars and soda pop. True, he won't drop dead within a few days of such an unhealthy diet, but his quality of life will be seriously impaired. The constant intake of sugar will gradually rot his teeth, deplete his overall energy level, and could even lead to something as serious as diabetes. Worse than that, by substituting healthy food with sweets, his body will not receive the nutrition that is required to ward off sickness and to sustain life. Undoubtedly, the results of such a lifestyle would be a sickly existence and an untimely death.

In the same way, a lifestyle centered around pleasurable experiences will rot out your spiritual life and possibly corrupt your soul. This isn't to say that pleasure doesn't have a place in the Christian's life. But pleasurable experiences are only meant to be the dessert of life. Kept in its proper perspective, pleasure is secondary to the staples of a healthy spiritual diet—which includes essentials like prayer, Bible reading, church attendance, deeds of kindness, giving of tithes and offerings, and so on. However, when gratification becomes the main focal point of one's daily existence, it has a way of choking out everything that is wholesome.

01 The Greek term for pleasure is *hedone*, from which we derive the term hedonism: "the doctrine that pleasure or happiness is the highest good; devotion to pleasure as a way of life."[i] Explain the difference between keeping pleasure in its proper perspective, and the "devotion to pleasure as a way of life."

Moses is one of the first biblical figures who pushed back on his natural desire for pleasure for the sake of his walk with God.

02 Read Hebrews 11:24-26.

A Explain in your own words how the choices he made lined up with the biblical definition of faith in Hebrews 11:1.

B What was it that motivated Moses to reject the pleasures of Egypt?

In His parable about the sower and the seed, Jesus used four qualities of soil to illustrate the various ways in which people respond to the Word of God. The first three soils produced no fruit and thus represent those who, at the end of the day, prove themselves unfaithful to the Lord.

03 Read Luke 8:14 and explain in your own words how each of these aspects of life would hinder a person from being faithful and fruitful.

A Worries/Cares

B Riches

C Pleasures

04 In James 4:1-5, James utters some piercing words to professing Christians among his readers who were addicted to pleasure. Read that passage and explain in your own words why they were in need of such warnings.

In 2 Timothy 3, Paul devoted five verses to describe the lifestyles of many professing Christians alive during the last days. The list begins with "lovers of self" in verse 2 and ends with "lovers of pleasure rather than lovers of God, holding to a form of godliness, although they have denied its power…" in verse 5.

05 As you look around you at the Church culture of our time, can you see how Paul's prediction is coming true? Read that passage in 2 Timothy 3 and describe what you see occurring today in light of it.

Reflection Questions

01 When you read 2 Timothy 3:1-5, which of those characteristics have you seen at work in your own life (in addition to viewing pornography)?

02 If you were transformed into someone who loves the things of God, how would your life change? Write out a portrait of the kind of person you want to become (with God's help).

The discipline of fasting is one tool that the Lord has provided for believers who have allowed themselves to become addicted to pleasure. As the man or woman develops the habit of abstaining from food for a period of time in order to devote themselves to prayer, Bible study or meeting other's needs, something powerful begins to happen. The course of their life begins to shift from one of self-indulgence and selfishness to one of giving and self-sacrifice. This turn of direction is described in Scripture as repentance.

Some people have embarked on a "special fast," hoping that this one act of self-denial will break the power of sin in their life. But fasting is not some magical act that will bring about immediate spiritual change in your life. It is the *practice* of self-denial which helps train the believer to stand against the desires of his flesh.

03   With that in mind, write out how you think fasting may help in your addiction to pornography.

☑ **Action Step**
Describe any plan you might make to begin a practice of regular fasting.

Day Complete ✓

Day Twelve

PRACTICE MAKES PERFECT

Will's Story (Graduated 2017)

Being bound in sexual sin for nearly 40 years and trying multiple methods to find freedom, I was all too familiar with Einstein's definition of insanity. However, by applying the principles set forth in God's Word, He brought me out! Fundamentals like a consistent daily quiet time (especially pushing through in the "dry seasons"), a sincere, deeper lifestyle of repentance and living in the light were definitely keys to the victory God has wrought for me.

As a child, I discovered that I possessed a very creative imagination and would often drift into a fantasy world to escape my unpleasant childhood. Upon reaching puberty I discovered pornography and masturbation, which only served to deepen my fantasy life. Fantasy, porn and masturbation became ever present companions in my life, even through two marriages.

At the age of 51, I was totally undisciplined, and my life was a mess. However, I knew my problem and its solution were both spiritual in nature. It was clear I needed radical change and radical HELP.

I entered the Pure Life Ministries Residential Program hoping it would help restore personal disciplines and spiritual practices that I had long since abandoned. I knew it was the Lord speaking to me through the staff so I did my best to respond humbly. I continually cried out to

God for deliverance from both my habitual sin and my very sin nature. I had to learn to repent for not only what I had done, but for who I was: an idolater, a sexual deviant, a drunkard, and especially a moral and spiritual coward.

I also quickly began to see the value of practicing a daily quiet time of prayer and Bible study. This new habit was not easy to establish because my job required me to clock-in at 6:00 a.m. This meant I had to begin my devotions by 3:30. As hard as it was, I was determined to persevere because I knew my life was on the line. Thankfully it became easier over time as both my body and mind became accustomed to the routine. In fact, it soon became a joy.

Along with a daily quiet time and ongoing repentance, I learned the necessity of being open and honest with my spiritual leaders about my struggles.

In my flesh, I wanted to hide my failures, as I had done throughout my life. But too much was at stake to go back into my old deceptive ways.

Another new habit I established at Pure Life was maintaining a gratitude journal. Writing down the many things I had to be thankful to the Lord for really helped me keep a positive attitude. Memorizing Scripture was another helpful addition to my daily routine. Getting the Word inside me strengthened my resolve to live a godly life.

I guess when I add up all the positive habits that I established, I would just sum it up by saying the Lord helped me develop a new lifestyle. The old sloppy life of indulgence was gone, and a new disciplined life took its place. I don't have the words to express what a blessing it has been to be living a godly life!

A Study in God's Word

Today's video, *Behind Sexual Sin Lies the Pleasure Hormone*, quoted Albert Einstein's famous quip: "The definition of insanity is doing the same thing over and over again, but expecting different results." As a scientist, he was primarily referring to scientific experiments, which are procedures "carried out to support or refute a hypothesis."[i] So Einstein could envision a fellow researcher mixing the exact same ingredients time after time in the hopes of arriving at a different conclusion. That really would be insane!

Now let's consider that reality in the life of someone involved in habitual sin. The person is tempted to commit a pleasurable sin. He yields to the temptation, but after it is all over he realizes that it did not deliver the level of satisfaction it seemed to promise. The insanity involved in his life is that he keeps falling for the temptation time after time in spite of knowing how little it would satisfy him. Not only will the experience prove to be unfulfilling, but he will also be forced to face the inevitable consequences that follow.

There are two Greek terms that describe human activity in the New Testament (NT): *prasso* and *poieo*. The term *poieo* refers to behavior that is occasionally performed; while the term *prasso* describes activity that is done repeatedly, habitually.

01 Each of the following verses employ the verb *prasso*. The adverb "habitually" is added to each instance to bring out the original meaning more clearly. Explain what you learn in each verse.

"For everyone who [habitually] <u>does</u> evil hates the Light, and does not come to the Light for fear that his deeds will be exposed."
John 3:20

"Do not marvel at this; for an hour is coming, in which all who are in the tombs will hear His voice, and will come forth; those who did the good deeds to a resurrection of life, those who [habitually] <u>committed</u> the evil deeds to a resurrection of judgment."
John 5:28-29

"I am afraid that when I come again my God may humiliate me before you, and I may mourn over many of those who have sinned in the past and not repented of the impurity, immorality and sensuality which they have [habitually] <u>practiced</u>."
2 Corinthians 12:21

"Now the deeds of the flesh are evident, which are: immorality, impurity, sensuality, idolatry, sorcery, enmities, strife, jealousy, outbursts of anger, disputes, dissensions, factions, envying, drunkenness, carousing, and things like these, of which I forewarn you, just as I have forewarned you, that those who [habitually] practice such things will not inherit the kingdom of God."
Galatians 5:19-21

The above verses describe God's sober perspective regarding sinful practices, but the opposite holds just as true. As I wrote in my book, *At the Altar of Sexual Idolatry*, "If we practice, (or sow) ungodliness then we will desire (or reap) ungodliness. By the same token, if we practice godliness, then we will desire a greater godliness. Feelings always follow behavior. The proper habits need to be established into our minds, and as they are, we will desire to continue in them."

02 Describe what you learn about habitually practicing good deeds from the following verses.

"…but kept declaring both to those of Damascus first, and also at Jerusalem and then throughout all the region of Judea, and even to the Gentiles, that they should repent and turn to God, [habitually] performing deeds appropriate to repentance."
Acts 26:20

"For we must all appear before the judgment seat of Christ, so that each one may be recompensed for his deeds in the body, according to what he has [habitually] done, whether good or bad."
2 Corinthians 5:10

"The things you have learned and received and heard and seen in me, [habitually] <u>practice</u> these things, and the God of peace will be with you."
Philippians 4:9

Reflection Questions

01   Looking back at the past 6 months, would you consider your pornography use to be more of an "occasional failure" or "habitual activity?" Write down your thoughts here.

02   Some of the passages you looked at in today's study are associated with judgment. Based on these Scriptures, what role will your habitual activities (rather than occasional ones) play on your Judgment Day?

03   Aside from sexual sin, list 5 ungodly activities that have become habitual in your life.

A   D

B   E

C

04   Take some time to consider these habitual patterns of sin and write out an honest confession to God for how you have habitually sinned against Him. Also, if you'd like to express the desire to repent of these things, now would be a good time to do that as well.

🕊 **Prayer Point**
Are there godly activities that you have begun recently (or need to begin) that you want to develop into habits? Pray over each activity and ask the Lord to help you persevere in these areas.

Day Complete ✓

Day Thirteen
STRONGHOLDS OF SIN

Watch Truth #7:
*Satan Wants to Plant a
Stronghold Inside You*

Brandon's Story (Graduated 2021)

Habitual sexual sin had hollowed out my life to the point where I felt like an utterly empty shell of a man. I no longer had any fruit of the Spirit: no joy, no love, no peace, no patience, no kindness, and certainly no self-control. In fact, all I had was a powerful self-life. My life-dominating habit of pornography had warped me into believing that it was my lot in life to continue onward in this cycle of sin and "repentance." Who was I even kidding? I got to the point where I was not even trying to repent and certainly not confessing my sins to a spiritual authority. I convinced myself that God "understood" and was okay with my sin.

I had been attending a charismatic church and Bible school, but sadly the outward emotional hype gave me a false sense of security, even glossing over any sense of guilt from my ongoing sin. Although I was oblivious to it, there was no substance left of any real spiritual life. This spiritual backsliding continued little by little after graduating from Bible school. I stopped reading the Word and gave up praying. I wasn't even listening to Christian music much anymore. Instead, I allowed more and more of the world to creep into my life until I lost all conviction of my sin. I was selfish, depressed, lonely, full of self-pity and miserable to be around.

The Lord had to humble me to the point of losing everything to get my attention. It was then that He brought me to the Pure Life Ministries Residential Program where I was able to cut off all connection to sin. I started reading the Word and praying every day. I also confessed my sin in its entirety. My desires began to shift; instead of seeing God as this distant being who permitted my sin, I saw Jesus as the one who was calling me to come to Him so I might truly be washed clean. He wasn't just offering me forgiveness; He was offering to allow me to participate in His love to the point where I wouldn't want my sin anymore. My life began to shift drastically from self-focus to seeking God with my whole heart. I knew full well that I was hopeless without His mercy. He began to fill me with His Spirit and began to heal those dark recesses I had kept walled off from everyone.

I had confessed my sin and knew that I had become a new creation in Christ. The old had surely passed away. As my time went on in the Residential Program, I started seeing the fruit of the Spirit being manifested to others as I released control of my life and allowed Jesus to reign.

A Study in God's Word

✍ Write out Romans 6:16.

01 Read and meditate on the Phillips translation of 2 Corinthians 10:3-5 provided below,[1] then answer the questions provided:

The truth is that, although of course we lead normal human lives, the battle we are fighting is on the spiritual level. The very weapons we use are not those of human warfare but powerful in God's warfare for the destruction of the enemy's strongholds. Our battle is to bring down every deceptive fantasy and every imposing defence that men erect against the true knowledge of God. We even fight to capture every thought until it acknowledges the authority of Christ.

---

1   This paraphrase is supplied because it brings out more clearly than the more literal translations what Paul was intending to communicate.

A Explain why human weapons are ineffective in the spiritual battles we face.

B What is the purpose of our battle?

C What is the ultimate aim of this struggle?

02 Make a list of false ideologies and religions that are prevalent in our culture.

A   D

B   E

C   F

03   Pick two of the ideologies or religions you listed and explain how they have presented a false view of God's character in our day and age.

A

B

Reflection Questions

01   Reflect on all that makes up the way you live your life (actions, thought patterns, emotions, etc.). In what areas of your life do you feel like you're out of control?

02   On Day 10, Question #2, you identified certain passionate desires that are very strong inside of you. Now, with those answers in mind, what do you think is the connection between those desires and the out-of-control behaviors in your life? Explain your reasoning.

Years ago, one of our staff members wrote an article called, "If it's Sin, There's Hope!" His point was that real freedom from our struggles will only come when we're willing to take full responsibility for them. Think about it: if my struggles are someone else's fault, then I'm doomed to remain stuck in sin. But if I am willing to admit that I'm in spiritual trouble because of *my own sin*, then I have tremendous hope, because Jesus Christ came to save sinners!

03   Using the things you listed above, write out a confession to the Lord where you take full responsibility for the spiritual strongholds in your life. This would be a good opportunity to get before the Lord to confess and repent of any known ongoing sins or any willful resistance to His authority.

☑ **Action Step**
If you haven't already set up a meeting to confess your sin to a trusted friend or spiritual authority, consider adding some of these out-of-control areas to your list of things to confess in that meeting.

Day Complete ✓

Day Fourteen

GOD'S HOLY PLACE

Alec's Story (Graduated 2022)

God knows. God understands. God forgives. Those were the lies I would tell myself during worship services in God's house. I experienced a great burden of guilt and anxiety while in church; overwhelming emotions that would condemn me and convince me that I wasn't saved. When I felt that way, I would plead for forgiveness and salvation repeatedly until I felt saved again. This made up my weekly Sunday ritual, often vacillating back and forth multiple times through a single service. I felt condemned over my sin. But then I would lie to myself, believing my remorse to be genuine and that I was forgiven in spite of the lack of confession or true repentance over my ongoing sin.

Each Sunday, I would go through the same battle as the guilt of the new sins of that week plagued me. But this would soon be followed by my own deceptive, emotion-driven thinking which convinced me that since I had been baptized and believed in God, that I was forgiven.

Looking back on that time, it's clear to me that the enemy was at work in the midst of all of this chaos as well, stimulating and energizing my anxieties. My reliance on unstable emotions made it possible for them to become a stronghold of deception inside me. My reality was based more on feelings than on truth, convincing myself that I was saved regardless of the fact that I was living in unrepentant sin.

At that point I did not understand that taking responsibility for my sin would lead to a life-changing repentance. Yes, it might be a painful path to take, but it would end in true hope for my soul. The fortress I built to protect myself from the truth was actually a hellish prison of torture. My prayers felt empty, my emotions plagued me, and my thoughts condemned me. It was as if I was locked in a room with a feral beast with no way to protect myself.

When God's conviction finally broke through my prison walls, the brokenness I experienced was not just an emotion of grief, but an overwhelming revelation of His love for me. The confession and subsequent exposure that I feared would destroy me, actually brought the cleansing I longed for. Forgiveness was no longer based on a fleeting emotion; it was a firm foundation and refuge. I could stand before the Lord, not in fear and anxiety, but in a peace that was enveloped in His love and mercy. My tormented soul was finally free!

A Study in God's Word

As you heard in the video, the real stronghold in your life is not a demon, it is sin. But if it is sin, then there is hope, because God has clearly laid out in Scripture how we can deal with it. One of the first steps is to come to grips with the emptiness of sin. The truth is that sin never delivers what it promises. So today, we want to look at the deceptive emptiness of the stronghold of lust.

01   Read and meditate on Psalm 24.

✍ **Write out Psalm 24:3-4.**

The word *shav* (used in v. 4) is employed 47 times in the Old Testament. About half the time it is translated with some form of the word "false," while in the rest of its occurrences it is used to describe some form of emptiness or vanity.

02 Read the following supplied verses that contain the underlined term *shav*. Write a brief statement for each verse explaining any new insights it gives you regarding the way this term is used in Psalm 24.

"Surely God will not listen to an <u>empty</u> cry, nor will the Almighty regard it."
Job 35:13

"I do not sit with <u>deceitful</u> men, nor will I go with pretenders."
Psalm 26:4

"I hate those who regard <u>vain</u> idols, but I trust in the LORD."
Psalm 31:6

"Turn away my eyes from looking at <u>vanity</u>, and revive me in Your ways."
Psalm 119:37

"Bring your <u>worthless</u> offerings no longer, incense is an abomination to Me. New moon and sabbath, the calling of assemblies—I cannot endure iniquity and the solemn assembly."
Isaiah 1:13

"Woe to those who drag iniquity with the cords of <u>falsehood</u>, and sin as if with cart ropes."
Isaiah 5:18

"Those who regard <u>vain</u> idols forsake their faithfulness."
Jonah 2:8

03 Read Matthew 5:27-30 and describe any similarities you see with it and Psalm 24:3-4. Also explain whether you see any allusion to lust, fantasy and masturbation in these two passages.

04 List the four promises listed in Psalm 24:3-5 for the one who "has clean hands and a pure heart," and "who has not lifted up his soul to *shav*."

A   C

B   D

Reflection Questions

Consider the following statement made in the video:
"It is clear that the enemy exploits the power of habit in a person by leading him back to his pet sin over and over again until the love of that sin is deeply entrenched within him."

01 How has the enemy capitalized on fantasies you have nurtured over the years?

We've worked with thousands of Christians over the years, many who felt that the strongholds in their lives could never be destroyed. But Jesus came to destroy the works of the devil! (1 John 3:8)

02 It's time to develop a strategy to guard yourself against the enemy's attempts to reinforce strongholds in your soul. Here is a list of petitions that should become a regular part of your prayer life.

- ◆ Destroy the enemy's strongholds that are inside me.
  Break every hold the enemy might have on my heart, and
  bring me into the freedom of the sons of God.
- ◆ Remove any spiritual blindness that may remain because of my
  involvement with sin and open my eyes to Your Truth.
- ◆ Tear down any vain thoughts and imaginations that remain
  in my mind. Destroy any false understandings about You
  and help me to see You for who You really are.
- ◆ Destroy the pride and lust that is still active in me.
  Establish in me a hatred of these sins.
- ◆ Teach me how to replace unbelief with true faith and intimate
  knowledge of You as You have revealed Yourself to be in Your Word.
- ◆ Build a foundation of truth and purity in my life.
- ◆ Bring my stubborn will into true submission. Teach my
  heart to love doing the things that please You.

Take some time right now to bring these petitions to the Lord.

03 Do you see anything you must do to cooperate with the Lord and facilitate the
answer to these prayers in your life?

☑ **Action Step**
As a way to remember to pray these prayers, write down any of them that
stood out to you and put them in a prominent place in your home. Pray them
whenever you see them!

Day Complete ✓

Day Fifteen

THE HUMAN HEART OF THE OLD TESTAMENT

Watch Truth #8:
Lust Begins in the Heart

Noah's Story (Graduated 2023)

One of the biggest spiritual breakthroughs I experienced occurred when the Lord opened my eyes to see the level of darkness that was active in my heart.

For almost a decade I had been indulging in sexual fantasy that became deeper and darker as the years went on. In the great love I had for my idol, I willingly allowed anything and everything into my heart in the attempt to please and gratify myself. Living this way led me into masturbation, porn and many very dark things. It got to the point where it became difficult to even have a conversation with someone without fantasizing about them. All of this was going on while I went to church and ran in Christian circles, maintaining the image of a "good Christian guy."

My two worlds often collided, and yet, after brief periods of freedom, I would always end up back in the same pit. No matter how hard I tried to abstain from sin I just couldn't do it. My dad had gone through the Pure Life Ministries Residential Program and when my secret sin was exposed yet again, he suggested that I go there also.

I reluctantly agreed to go, but I arrived there in a great deal of delusion about my spiritual condition. I regularly entertained thoughts such as: "I'm not as bad as my dad;" "Everyone else's problems are a lot worse than mine;" or "At least I didn't go as far as others." I just thought very highly of myself.

My prideful attitude began to change one day when the Lord used Matthew 5:27-30 to show me that in His eyes I was just as guilty for my fantasies as if I had actually participated in them. That put an end to my excuse, "It's only fantasy."

He opened my eyes to see that the reason I had never been able to overcome sexual sin was that I had always focused on trying to change my outward behavior instead of allowing Him to deal with my heart. My heart remained untouched, which is why I would return to my sin time and time again. I came to understand that my behavior was determined by the thoughts I allowed to persist in my heart—whether for good or for bad.

This all came to a culmination point for me when I confessed to my counselor what was really going on inside me. It was the first time in my life that I dealt with the source of all my problems: my heart.

Since that first turning to the Lord, He has continually helped me to guard my heart and deal with sin there at ground zero before allowing it to go any further. I am now living in victory through a relationship with Jesus Christ that I have never known or experienced before.

A Study in God's Word

The human heart is the core of a person's life. It is that part of our inner man that sets the tone for all one's desires, the decisions those desires drive, the lifestyle that results in one's choices and ultimately one's eternal destiny. No wonder spiritual forces—both good and evil—fight to be in a position to influence a person's heart!

✍ Write out Proverbs 4:23.

01 Look up the following verses and briefly write out in your own words what you learn about the functions and attributes of the human heart.

📖 1 Kings 11:3

📖 Psalm 66:18

📖 2 Chronicles 12:14

📖 Psalm 119:2

📖 Psalm 37:4

📖 Psalm 119:11

📖 Psalm 51:10

📖 Proverbs 3:5

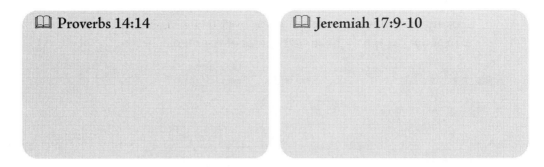

📖 Proverbs 14:14

📖 Jeremiah 17:9-10

In the previous verses, one of the things we discover is that our hearts will be changed based on what we give ourselves to. If we give ourselves over to wickedness, then the result will be that our spiritual life will dry up and our carnal nature will become increasingly inflamed. On the other hand, if we pursue the things of God, our spiritual life will grow more vibrant and our carnal nature will become more diminished.

02　King David would have understood all this very well. He had a good grasp on what it meant to be devoted to God and also what it meant to have his heart corrupted by sin. Read what he said in 1 Chronicles 28:9 where he is giving a charge to his son Solomon.

A　In your own words, explain what you think David meant when he told Solomon:

1　To serve God with a "whole heart"

2　To serve God with a "willing mind"

B   In your own words, write the two conditional promises (one positive and one negative) David made to his son.

1

2

03   Despite a good start, and incredible wisdom, Solomon still got off track in his walk with the Lord. Read 1 Kings 11:1-8 and explain in your own words where Solomon went wrong in life.

04   How would you compare the path you have taken with what Solomon experienced?

Reflection Questions

01   If our actions have the power to influence and shape our hearts over time, how do you think each of the following actions would change a person's heart? Journal your thoughts in the space provided.

A   Deceiving other people

B   Praying for a need in someone else's life

C   Practicing self-denial

D   Giving thanks to the Lord no matter what is going on in your life

E   Spending quality time in God's Word

F   Obeying what you read in God's Word

G   Refusing to admit that you're wrong

H   Watching television that has cursing, violence or sex

I   Pursuing wealth or fame

J   Being jealous of what others have

At this point in your life, it's probably easy to feel like evil influences are very strong inside of you, and the good is weak and frail. Don't give up! As you respond to God's truth, you will begin to see the power of evil losing its hold on you, and your heart will begin to be shaped by the things of God.

☑ **Action Step**

As you go throughout your day, make a real effort to obey God in the little things, and believe that He will change your heart over time. If you fail, acknowledge it to the Lord and keep going!

Day Complete ✓

Day Sixteen

THE HUMAN HEART OF THE NEW TESTAMENT

Cody's Story (Graduated 2020)

My problems with sexual sin began at a young age watching television. It was obvious that women's bodies were pleasing to men, and I wanted in on that pleasure and excitement for myself.

Throughout my school years I developed a practice of going to the local library and using the internet for "schoolwork," while I was actually using it to visit porn sites. Each time I got away with this I went into darker pornography to see how far I could go and if the pleasure would increase. Over time I ended up drawn into sites focused on sexual violence and BDSM.

Eventually I got married, and things began looking up when we had our first child. I had a family now, what could

go wrong? What went wrong was that my desire for illicit pleasure continued to thrive inside me. I soon returned to pornography. Things got so bad that I developed a daily habit of watching it in the restroom at work.

It was at this point that I started entertaining a fantasy about having an affair. This was helped along by visiting adult sites that facilitated married people hooking up with others. At the time this just seemed like another fantasy.

Coincidentally, our church leadership asked us to join three other families in a church plant outreach to a poor neighborhood. The eight of us became very close to the point that hanging out at each other's houses was normal. One of the other wives and I clicked together really well, often using our quick-witted sarcasm to pick on other friends. This was all the familiarity I needed for me to start plugging her into my adultery fantasies.

About two years into the church plant, she sent me a happy birthday text which opened the door to a number of texts going back and forth between us over the next couple of days. Communicating back-to-back days was unprecedented in how we had interacted up till then. This was exciting for me because her messages started to show her hand throughout the day and ultimately ended with her stating that she wanted something she couldn't have. I replied that she would be surprised what she could have if she simply asked. That was it; that started a two-month relationship involving hours of phone conversations, thousands of text messages and me visiting her house while her husband was at work.

It lasted only a month before everything came out and my marriage fell apart. After reading about the adulteress in Proverbs 6, the Lord convicted me that something needed to change inwardly. Eventually I landed at the Pure Life Ministries Residential Program where I learned to fight for, keep, and protect my heart. My personal testimony is that a heart set on Jesus is always full and will fight to preserve one's relationship with Him.

A Study in God's Word

Yesterday we discussed what the Old Testament reveals about the human heart. Today we will look at what the New Testament has to say. Some people have said that in the OT God was primarily concerned with outward behavior, while in the NT He is primarily concerned with the inner life. While there is some validity to this, the truth is that He has always been concerned with people's hearts because they affect a person's behavior and ultimately his destiny. No wonder He emphasizes the need for a pure heart! Keep that in mind as you complete today's study.

✍ Write out 2 Timothy 2:22.

01 Look up the following verses and write out in your own words what you learn about the functions and attributes of the heart. Just as a reminder, you would do well to remember that because of what Jesus accomplished on the cross, the grace of God is available to help you live a life pleasing to the Lord.

📖 Matthew 5:8

📖 Mark 7:21

📖 Matthew 5:28

📖 Luke 21:34

📖 Matthew 6:21

📖 Romans 1:21-25

📖 Matthew 15:8

📖 Romans 2:5

📖 Hebrews 3:12

This might be a good spot to interject something that James said as a reminder that, while God is always available to help His children in their spiritual battles, we have our part to play as well. The men in our Residential Program are often told, "we initiate, God empowers." That statement sheds some light on the unseen interaction that goes on between a believer and God as he battles the temptation to sin.

02   Read James 4:8 and explain in your own words what it says about our part in this struggle.

03   You've looked up a lot of verses in the past two days that spoke about the heart. Review what you wrote down from these passages and write a paragraph of not less than 250 words describing the important role the human heart plays in a person's spiritual journey.

Reflection Questions

01 Take some time to consider the reality of your daily life (how you spend your time, money and attention). What does this reveal to you about your heart?

02 Imagine that the desires in your heart became more and more godly. How would this change the reality of your daily life?

☑ **Action Step**
As was mentioned above, "we initiate, God empowers." Your desire to live a new life is a good desire, but it will only be realized as you learn to obey God in faith. As an act of faith, believing that God is able to change your heart, what will you do differently today?

Day Complete ✓

Day Seventeen

GOD'S DISCIPLINE PRODUCES THE FEAR OF THE LORD

Watch Truth #9:
The Fear of the Lord is the Beginning of Wisdom

Daniel's Story (Graduated 2019)

I remember the day I confessed my secret sin to my pastor. It was probably the most terrifying moment I had ever experienced at that point. But looking back, I see God's hand in my life disciplining me and bringing me to Himself. Because I went through that difficult situation, I have something in Christ I wouldn't trade for anything.

One of the reasons that confession was so frightening was because I had convinced everyone around me that I was a great guy. Not only was I excelling in my career, but I was also beginning to fulfill numerous ministry opportunities at church. Nobody would have guessed what was really going on inside me, though. I felt totally isolated from others. I hated myself and was constantly critical of others. I was obsessed with pleasure and could hardly resist the urge to give over to porn, fantasy and masturbation several times a day.

What got me into my pastor's office was the overwhelming burden of guilt I was carrying. Coming clean with my spiritual leader was somewhat of a relief, but I still had to face the painful devastation that came as a result of the consequences of my sin.

My pastor was shocked to learn that the person he thought I was differed greatly from reality. I thought when I confessed to him that he would comfort me and pity me; instead, he offered stern rebukes and gave me difficult things I needed to do.

For one, I was told I should quit my job. Even more challenging was being instructed to get help somewhere, preferably the Pure Life Ministries Residential Program. I defended myself, saying that his reaction wasn't justified since I hadn't acted out on any of my fantasies. His response was that my inner world and fantasy life were just as bad as acting out in reality. I hadn't crossed any physical lines, but I had crossed lines in my heart.

My thinking about sexual sin totally changed as I began to accept the truth of what he was saying. I did end up going to Pure Life Ministries, but if I thought that everything would change the minute I stepped on the property I was in for a rude awakening. At first, it seemed that my lustful thoughts were worse than ever. Looking back I realize it just seemed that way because it was the first time in my

life I had ever tried to resist them. I was determined though and became resolute that I would not give an inch in indulging them. That came, to a large degree, because of the painful experience I had been through. God's discipline, through my pastor, showed me that lust in the heart is just as sinful to God as lust acted upon.

The wonderful news is that today I live in victory over sexual sin. I don't struggle with temptation to give over, and I am not plagued with lustful thoughts like I once was. And more than that, I have joy and peace and a desire to love God and others that I never had before. The discipline of God seemed almost too much to bear in my life when my world came crashing down around me. But He was faithful to see me through that process and to bring me into a real life with Himself.

A Study in God's Word

One of the worst side effects of porn addiction is that it trains us to live a lifestyle characterized by instant gratification and selfish indulgence. At some point, those who plan on living a genuine Christian life must come to grips with this un-Christlike way of living and face their need for change. But acknowledging one's need is only the beginning. Real change will only come about as a person submits to the processes of God's discipline—this and this alone will enable him to live a holy life in the midst of a decadent and perverse society.

Scripture has much to say about the concept of discipline. *Chastisement, reproof, warning, correction, instruction* and *training* are all terms used under the general theme of discipline in the Bible. These may not be popular terms in our "anything goes" culture, but collectively they describe the way God deals with His children in all ages.

01 Read the following verses and briefly describe why human beings are in need of God's discipline.

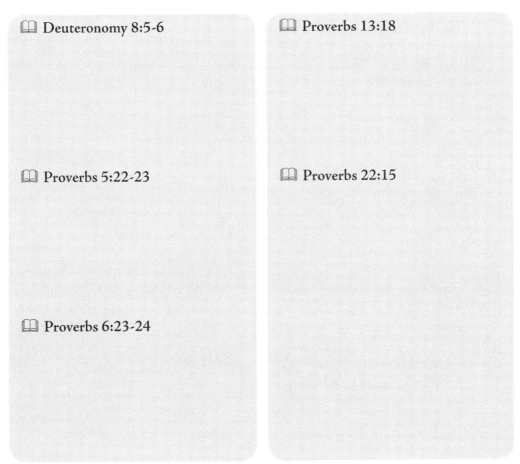

📖 Deuteronomy 8:5-6

📖 Proverbs 13:18

📖 Proverbs 5:22-23

📖 Proverbs 22:15

📖 Proverbs 6:23-24

During nearly 40 years of ministry, the Pure Life counselors have encountered countless men who have made numerous attempts to break free from the vicious grip of pornography but with no success. Why? Because the vast majority of them were looking for quick, convenient and pain-free solutions.

Truthfully, there is no such solution. Men who are determined to find the easy way are simply wasting precious time groping around for what does not exist. *A life which becomes out of control only comes back under control through the painful processes of God's discipline.*

02 The following verses describe these processes, and the good that comes into the lives of those who submit. Look up the verses and then write a small, summarizing paragraph describing what you can expect to happen in your own life if you submit to God's discipline.

📖 Job 5:17-18   📖 Isaiah 48:10
📖 Psalm 119:67   📖 Hebrews 5:7-8

03 The writer of Hebrews understood both the necessity and the difficulty of enduring the discipline of the Lord in a profitable way. Read Hebrews 12:4-13 and answer the following questions:

A   What does this passage teach us about God's heart for us as He disciplines us?

B   How have your perspectives of God's discipline been different from what is portrayed in this passage?

C   How must we handle God's discipline if it is going to profit us spiritually?

◻ What response to God's discipline could cause us to suffer spiritually?

Reflection Questions

01 Read Proverbs 9:7-8. Which of the men depicted has more accurately described your response to God's dealings with you in the past? Give some examples from your own life.

02 Do you anticipate your response to the Lord to be the same or different in the future? Explain your answer.

🕊 Prayer Point
Regardless of how well or poorly you have done in the past, be assured that God loves you and greatly desires to help you. But if your life is going to change, you must allow Him to do His work in your heart. People don't change simply because they learn some things; they change when they respond to the Lord's dealings with them. Perhaps this would be a good opportunity for you to talk this over with the Lord. Let Him know that you are willing to do whatever it takes to become a godly person.

Day Complete ✓

Day Eighteen

THE VALUE OF THE FEAR OF THE LORD

Thomas' Story (Graduated 2006)

There was a time in my life when I did not fear God at all, and my whole life was one big mass of sin and corruption. I could look at porn and give over to my lusts daily with little to no concern over what God thought of my actions. I was a fool, living only for today.

My only desire was for pleasure with no thought of eternity and the long-term consequences of my sinful choices. I had become so corrupt that even my language was filthy and vile. In just opening my mouth others would be contaminated by vulgar words that expressed the sinful thoughts that filled my wicked heart.

For a time I was completely devoid of any conviction over my sin. Not only did I not fear God, but for a season in my life I lived as if good were evil and evil were good. I lived in the cesspool of sexual sin and loved to have it so. My highest goal in life was to satisfy my carnal desires. I glutted myself not only on porn, but also entertainment and food, anything that gratified my lust for pleasure and indulged my flesh. The constant cry of my heart was more, more, more!

Although I did not fear God, at times the truth I had suppressed for so long would nag at my soul. I grew up with a sense of right and wrong and with a conscience sensitive to evil. I had attended church and was taught the fear of the Lord; I just never embraced it. I was running from God, unwilling to fear Him, acknowledge Him, or submit to His authority over my life.

I am so thankful that this was not the end of my story. God in His mercy intervened in my life and gradually brought me to my senses. I started seeking God and made a half-hearted commitment to the Lord. I was still double-minded, so although my sin was not as all-encompassing as it had been in the past, I never found true and lasting victory.

However, the fear of the Lord *was* slowly beginning to develop in my heart. Eventually it became overwhelming. I knew something drastic needed to happen in my life. I knew I couldn't live this way anymore! It was then that God brought me to the Pure Life Ministries Residential Program. It was there He instilled within me a deep, abiding and genuine fear of God that became a catalyst to true change and freedom from sin in my life.

Since this time my life has changed dramatically, and a lot of it has happened because the Lord has become very real to me. The reality of His presence has brought about a strong desire not to do anything that would displease Him. No, I haven't arrived yet, but I now have a life of freedom that I never knew before. In His grace and mercy, the Lord has not only brought me into freedom but is also keeping me in freedom as I have chosen to embrace the fear of God in my life.

A Study in God's Word

When men think too little of God, they become high-minded and arrogant toward Him. It isn't long before they develop the attitude that He owes them eternal life and that obedience isn't really necessary. Just like the fear of danger is of enormous help to us in life, so too a healthy fear of God keeps a person from straying off track and into sin.

✍ Write out Isaiah 66:2b.

01 Read the following verses from Proverbs and briefly describe the benefits of fearing the Lord.

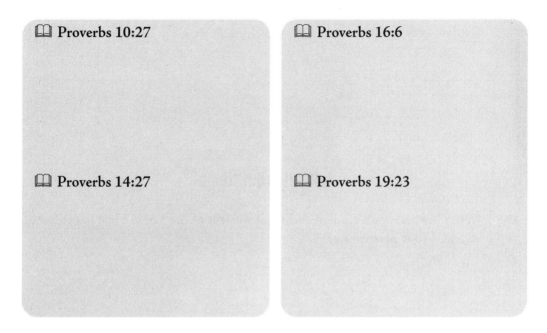

📖 Proverbs 10:27

📖 Proverbs 16:6

📖 Proverbs 14:27

📖 Proverbs 19:23

02 Take a moment and reflect on what you wrote down. Do you see your own need for these benefits in your life?

03 Keeping in mind everything you just read, rewrite 2 Corinthians 7:1 in your own words.

04 Explain in your own words what you think Paul meant in Philippians 2:12.

05   Explain in your own words what you think Peter meant in 1 Peter 1:17.

Reflection Questions

01   What has been your understanding of the fear of the Lord? How has this study changed your perspective?

02   Consider the life you have led to this point. Would you say that you have walked in the fear of the Lord? Explain your answer.

03 How would a healthy fear of the Lord affect the following aspects of your life?

A The way you treat people who are difficult to love.

B The way you act when no one is looking.

C How you handle yourself at your workplace.

Day Complete ✓

Day Nineteen

THE FOOL OF THE BIBLE

Watch Truth #10:
*The Root of Sexual
Addiction Probably Isn't
What You Think it is*

Alex's Story (Graduated 2017)

One would think that anyone in their right mind who faced expulsion from college, threats of arrest and harassment charges would have come to their senses and stopped the behavior that was bringing about all this trouble. But that was the issue; I was not in my right mind. My selfish desire for pleasure had turned me into a raging fool bent on satisfying every sexual desire, no matter the cost. I hadn't started out this way, though.

In the beginning stages of discovering sexual sin, I actually feared getting caught. The thought of someone thinking of me as a pervert kept me from getting into a lot of things that the other kids my age were regularly indulging in. But the more that I gave over to fantasy and masturbation, the stronger the desire became to actually experience those fantasies. And when I did finally have that physical encounter I found it to be everything I had imagined it to be. Now I wanted more.

As more opportunities came for me to indulge in the sin I craved, I gradually began to throw caution to the wind and started crossing lines I never would have imagined. It didn't matter who the person was or how foolish my actions might be, I was determined to gratify my every desire.

I should add that there were people in my life who were trying to talk sense to me. There were times when I was disciplined, counseled, warned, threatened and even begged to quit my behavior; none of it stopped me. Words simply couldn't change my thinking or penetrate my insanity. I had laid out a path that I was determined to see through—or so I thought.

One night, I was sitting in my Saturn coupe in a nearby city. I had just given over to sexual sin yet again, but this time it was different. Not only was it not satisfying, it left me feeling ashamed and disgusted with myself. It was in that moment that the Lord gave me a brief glimpse into where my sin was taking me. It was just enough to snap me out of my insanity. Here I was, this skinny 27-year-old guy sitting by myself in my car in the middle of the night in a seedy area of downtown.

In that moment, I felt so vulnerable and so alone. But what hit me the hardest was that I knew beyond a shadow of a doubt, that if someone came up and shot me or stabbed me I would go straight to hell. As fear began to overwhelm me I knew what I needed to do. I picked up my phone and called my pastor's son and confessed everything! Looking back, that day was the beginning of my path out of not only bondage to sexual sin, but the insanity of reckless abandonment to living life my way.

A Study in God's Word

A fool could be said to be someone who is controlled by his passions, regardless of what the consequences might be. Foolishness, then, could be defined as the amoral or immoral behavior of one who does not hold to God's moral standards and lacks the spiritual capacity to learn from the consequences of sin. Perhaps this would be a good time to consider the effects pornography has had on your life and on your relationships with others.

✍ Write out Psalm 107:17.

01 Some people seem to spend their lives going around and around the same mountain, never progressing in life, never understanding why they can't make headway. Look up the following verses about fools and describe what you learn from each.

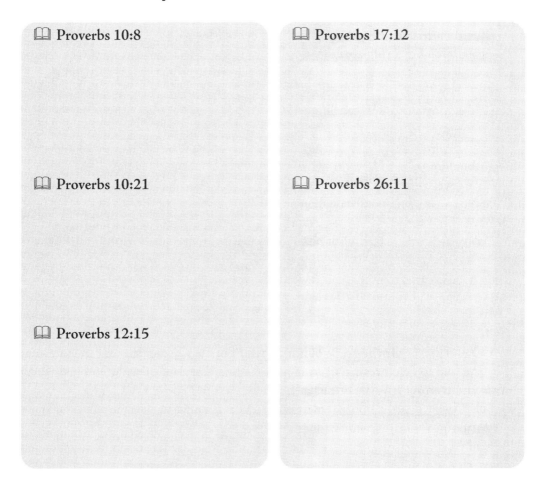

📖 Proverbs 10:8

📖 Proverbs 17:12

📖 Proverbs 10:21

📖 Proverbs 26:11

📖 Proverbs 12:15

02 Another truth about foolish people is that they disdain discipline—even God's corrective measures. Read the following verses and write what you learn about the fool and/or discipline.

📖 Job 5:17

📖 Psalm 50:16-17

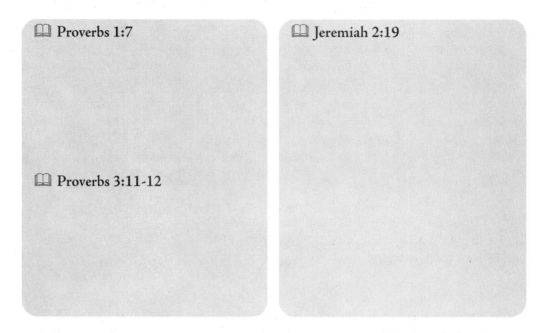

📖 Proverbs 1:7

📖 Jeremiah 2:19

📖 Proverbs 3:11-12

03   Proverbs 5 tells the story of a man who pursued sexual sin and the aftermath he had to face because of it. It really is like a picture of what you just read in Jeremiah 2:19. Write out what Solomon says in Proverbs 5:12-14.

Can you relate to the man in Solomon's story? Has your sin cost you more than you could have imagined? Proverbs 14:9 in the NASB and the NKJV says, "Fools mock at sin…" The ESV translates it, "Fools mock at the guilt offering…" Either way, the attitude of a foolish person is to make light of the seriousness of transgressing God's laws.

04   Explain the attitude you have exhibited in the past regarding pornography.

Reflection Questions

01 In what ways have you not taken seriously God's counsel or laws? What were the consequences?

02 In what ways have you avoided the pain of God's discipline?

03 Read Hebrews 12:11. What is the promise given to us if we submit to God's discipline?

04 What, if anything, have you resolved to do differently? What heart attitude or posture will you now take toward God's Word?

Day Complete ✓

Day Twenty

LOVE VS. LUST

Marcus' Story (Graduated 2020)

From my earliest days I was convinced that my strong desire for intimacy and love could only be fulfilled through a woman. This faulty thinking became further entrenched within me when I discovered internet pornography in middle school. Over the years I continued to indulge in porn, and although I also had numerous hookups, none of them satisfied my longing for intimacy.

In my early twenties, I had an encounter with the love of God that led me to take my spiritual life seriously for a season. During that time the thought actually came to me that this desire for meaningful love would only be found in Jesus, but this idea ran counter to what I had always believed.

I eventually did enter a serious relationship with a girl. Instead of leading me into the unselfishness of true love, the intimacy we shared simply made way for me to become even more selfish. For instance, I demanded that she satisfy my every desire. When I didn't get my way, I would become manipulative. By the time the relationship ended, any desire to know God was gone, and I was convinced that the answer to all my cravings for true love would only be found in illicit sexual sin.

What followed were numerous unsatisfying affairs. The further I went down this road, the emptier and uglier I became inside. It seemed that nothing could fill the black hole in my heart. In fact, the more I tried, the more hollowed out I felt.

It wasn't until I really hit bottom that I reached out for help. One of the things my counselor at Pure Life taught me was that a believer will only experience love when he becomes a channel of God's love to others. This also contradicted my long-held notion that I needed others to love me in order to feel loved.

By this point I was beginning to realize that my thinking must be off so I decided to do my best to live out what I was being taught. It started in small ways, like interceding for the needs of others instead of only praying for myself. It progressed from there to being helpful to other people when I saw a need. The more good deeds I did for others, the more my heart changed. I was gradually becoming a different person.

Over time I could tell that the Lord was purifying my heart. My whole life had been dominated by covetousness and idolatry. Those passions were being replaced by a love for God and others. The love and intimacy I had always sought became an integral part of my daily life. It became very real to me that the Lord truly did love me, and that He is the love, peace and stability I had been thirsting for all of my life. I've gone through many valleys, mountaintops and dull times since then, but His love has carried me through it all.

A Study in God's Word

Sin is always concerned with satisfying some lust of the flesh. It is the self-life asserting its desires over one's obligation to obey God's commandments. The more a person sins, the stronger that particular sin will become in his or her life. This pathway into habitual sin is what the enemy is constantly looking to encourage and foster.

Since sin is selfish by nature, the antidote to it must be unselfishness. But when a person is habitually indulging in sin, doing unselfish deeds seems impossible. He has given and given and given of himself to feed this monster of lust inside. When he sees what he's become and attempts to live unselfishly, he finds that he has nothing left for anyone else.

Nevertheless, one of the primary ways out of that pit of self-centered living is to begin to do unselfish deeds. The Bible calls this sort of behavior love (Greek-*agapé*).

✍ Write out 1 John 4:7-8.

01 Perhaps the best biblical definition of *agapé* is the Golden Rule. Read Matthew 7:12-14. Jesus was connecting the concept of unselfishness with the "narrow way" of true Christianity while linking the "broad way" to living for self. Answer the following questions.

A Which path do you feel applies to someone who has indulged in a constant fare of pornography? Explain your answer.

B Describe any changes you think would occur in your life if it was lived more in line with the Golden Rule.

02 Look up the following verses and briefly explain what you learn about *agapé* and how it should apply to your life as a follower of Christ.

📖 Mark 12:31

📖 Luke 6:32

📖 Luke 6:35

📖 John 13:35

📖 1 Corinthians 13:1-3

📖 Galatians 5:13

📖 1 Peter 4:8

Reflection Questions

01 Below, is a list of the seven Beatitudes and their opposites, as mentioned in the video. Spend some time meditating on each of them.

- "Blessed are the poor in spirit … and miserable are those who are full of themselves."
- "Blessed are those who mourn … and miserable are those who strive after temporal happiness."
- "Blessed are the meek … and miserable are the self-willed, who always want their way."
- "Blessed are those who hunger and thirst after righteousness … and miserable are those who are indifferent and apathetic to the things of God."
- "Blessed are the merciful … and miserable are the self-centered who never reach out to meet the needs of others."
- "Blessed are the pure in heart … and miserable are those whose hearts are full of idols."
- "Blessed are the peacemakers … and miserable are the troublemakers who cause division."

02 Hopefully this list has helped you to see the stark contrast between the blessed life of *living for God and others* and the miserable life of *living for self*. What are some of the greatest ways you need to change in order to come into a truly blessed life?

Prayer Point

Spend some time before the Lord, confessing how great your need to change is, and asking Him for the strength to walk in the pathway of the Beatitudes.

☑ **Action Step**

If your life has been lived in a spirit of intense selfishness, it's going to take time to learn how to live in a spirit of love. That being said, you need to begin doing acts of love *now*. Pick one of the activities below and begin regularly implementing it into your life.

Sacrifice some portion of your financial resources (beyond your tithe) and use it to meet other's needs (see 1 John 3:16-17).

Sacrifice some portion of your physical strength to help someone. Perhaps you could split wood for someone or rake their lawn (see Philippians 2:4).

Sacrifice some portion of your time and spend it with lonely and unloved people (see Ephesians 5:16).

Day Complete ✓

Now, let's add some new commitments. Remember, freedom from pornography comes about as you establish a completely different lifestyle.

☐ I will establish a consistent prayer life.

Later in this study, we will devote two days to explaining why a prayer life is vital for someone who wants to overcome sexual sin. But what is most important today is for you to get one started. I suggest that you make a commitment to pray ten minutes every morning for starters. Here are a few practical decisions you will need to make so that your prayer life works for you.

1   First, *when* will you pray? The best time of the day is before the hustle and bustle begins, so make sure you're waking up early enough to be with God before you get drawn into other things.

2   Second, *where* will you pray? Find a place in your house or dorm that lends itself to having quality time with God. (You may find it easier to walk and pray. Others may enjoy journaling or typing their prayers.)

3   Third, *what* will you pray about? There are many different methods of prayer, but perhaps a good way to start would be to remember the acrostic ACTS (Adoration, Confession, Thanksgiving, Supplication) and include each of these elements when you pray. You could also consider making a list of various groups of people to pray for (church, family, coworkers, classmates, etc.) on different days of the week.

4   Fourth, perhaps you would find it helpful to have someone who can help keep you accountable with your commitment. If this would be beneficial to you, find someone that you can text each day until the habit is established.

☐ **I will start a gratitude journal.**

There is a reason why so many of the psalms tell us to give thanks. Not only does God deserve our gratitude, but gratitude also benefits us in numerous ways. When we cultivate grateful hearts, we are putting up a spiritual shield that protects us from the many sins the enemy uses to lead us into lust (anger, self-pity, discontentment, despair, boredom, etc.). Each morning, express genuine gratitude to God for five to ten things in your life.

☐ **I will initiate a plan to begin spending quality time with my wife and/or other believers.**

One of the horrible side-effects of using pornography is that we become isolated, self-centered and disconnected from other believers. This makes us an easy target for the enemy. As you move forward on this journey, select a number of godly believers that you feel comfortable with (include your wife if you're married). Then, initiate a plan to begin having genuine, meaningful fellowship with them on a consistent basis.

Day Twenty-One

FORM WITHOUT SUBSTANCE

Watch Truth #11:
A Form of Godliness Does Not Have the Power to Deliver From Sin

Ian's Story (Graduated 2017)

I was twelve years old when I had my first real encounter with the Lord. Oh, I was raised in the church alright and had a basic understanding of Christianity. But I was already addicted to sexual sin and knew I was in trouble.

So late one evening, I decided I would acknowledge my sin to the Lord and ask Him to forgive me. God met me in that prayer by lifting the weight of my sin off my heart. Instantly, I felt like a new person! My heart leapt with joy in the knowledge that all my sins were forgiven.

That's when I heard the quiet voice, *"Will you give your life to me?"* Instantly, fear choked me. I knew that God was speaking to me. "What if God calls me to be a missionary or a pastor, or to be single?" I was afraid that if I opened my heart and surrendered my life to Him, God would make my life miserable. I went to sleep, annoyed that my newfound peace had been disturbed.

Within months, I was back to my old ways. I decided to quench the conviction of sin and act like everything was okay. I built a spotless reputation of integrity and diligence in my studies at school. Throughout my teenage years, I spent hours discussing the Bible with elders in my church and showed genuine interest in pursuing a deeper relationship with the Lord. I even had encounters with the Lord during this time where I felt His presence in a tangible way. Yet while I cultivated this spiritual image outwardly, I was spiraling into deeper sexual fantasies than ever before.

I was left in hopeless confusion by this dichotomy in my heart. On one hand I felt like I was growing in my love for God and the Bible. Yet, on the other hand, my sin was quickly getting out of control. Things couldn't continue this way.

At this point, I found Pure Life Ministries and decided I would enter the Residential Program. After I arrived, I slowly began to realize how I had deceived myself and others into thinking that I loved Jesus. The truth was that my lack of

surrender proved that I really didn't love Him. This was a tremendous revelation to me. Patiently, the Lord led me back to the place He had first spoken to me. This time I said, "Yes, Lord, I surrender my life completely to you."

This act of surrender—and the many that came after—opened the path of victory to me. I now live in the power of Jesus Christ over sexual temptation when it comes my way because my life is no longer my own. This life of surrender has broken down the walls of false spirituality and now allows the power of God to flow into my life.

A Study in God's Word

One of the most frightful aspects of Christianity is that it is possible to take on the outward characteristics of the Christian life without possessing the inward reality. Some people are raised in Christian homes and learn to act like Christians. Others go to church primarily to escape hell. Still others have had an emotional experience they have mistakenly considered a conversion. All of these people have one thing in common: they lack the life of God in their inner man. They may do many right things, but their heart has never been transformed.

✍ Write out 2 Timothy 3:5.

01 Each of the following verses reveal an aspect of what it looks like when people have "a form of godliness." Read each verse and explain what you learn.

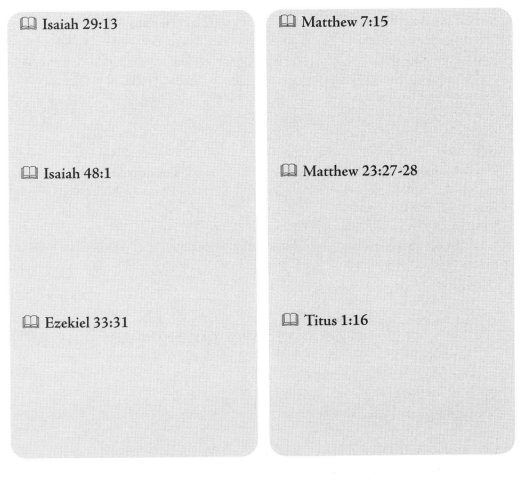

Isaiah 29:13

Isaiah 48:1

Ezekiel 33:31

Matthew 7:15

Matthew 23:27-28

Titus 1:16

02 Look up the following verses and describe what you learn about the characteristics of "the power of God."

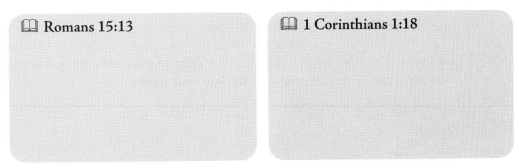

Romans 15:13

1 Corinthians 1:18

☑ SECOND CHECK-IN

Congratulations on persevering to the mid-point of this battle to overcome your addiction to pornography! Actually, this is a battle that will, to some degree, be with you the rest of your life. But don't worry—as you begin having victories, I promise it will become increasingly easier.

And speaking of that, let's consider where you are—or, at least, where you should be by now. At this point, you should be having some victories over temptation. You needn't be overly concerned if you're losing more of these spiritual skirmishes than you're winning. It's to be expected as you continue to lay the spiritual foundation upon which future victories will be won. You're still pretty new to fighting this battle God's way. Just keep fighting!

Alright, let's look at the commitments you should have implemented from Check-In 1.

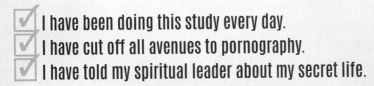

☑ I have been doing this study every day.
☑ I have cut off all avenues to pornography.
☑ I have told my spiritual leader about my secret life.

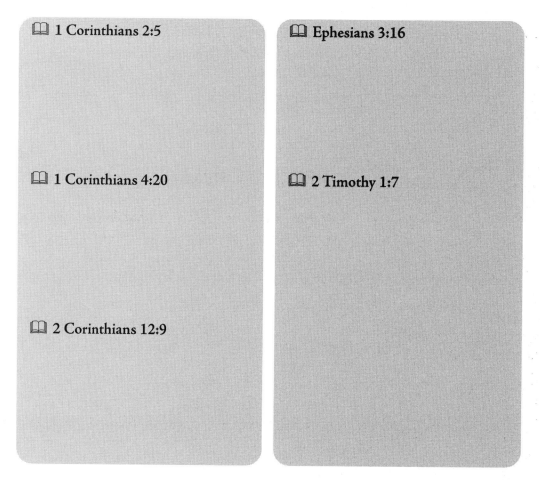

📖 1 Corinthians 2:5

📖 Ephesians 3:16

📖 1 Corinthians 4:20

📖 2 Timothy 1:7

📖 2 Corinthians 12:9

These verses reveal incredible promises about the power of God—hope, faith, strength, fearlessness and self-control. These are the exact things a porn addict needs if he is to overcome his bondage to sin. But these verses also describe how only a real life in Christ will bear such wonderful, powerful fruit.

03   Can you see that when all a man has is a "form of godliness," he will not have what he needs to overcome his sin? Explain your response.

Reflection Questions

01 Based on what you've learned over the past 20 days, what do you believe are the main reasons the power to change has been absent in your life?

02 What do you believe needs to change for God's power to be realized in your life?

🕊 **Prayer Point**
Take some time to pray through Colossians 3:5-14 and ask the Lord to help you develop a life of true godliness.

Day Complete ✓

Day Twenty-Two
ETERNAL LIFE

Jose's Story (Graduated 2016)

When I first discovered the realm of pornography, it seemed to be offering me a wonderful and exciting new life. Instead, what I received was nothing but misery. This was bad enough, but my misguided efforts to make up for my secret sin only led me into an outward form of godliness. And yet these efforts left me thinking that I really was walking with God in spite of the fact that I had no power to overcome sin.

I made a profession of faith and was baptized at a young age and was sure that this secured my entrance into heaven. Growing up I attended services, went to church camp, and even did mission trips. However, this "form of godliness" was only being lived out in front of church, family and friends. Secretly I had a life of hidden sin.

Years of bondage to pornography eventually led to sexual encounters. Nevertheless, I was convinced that attending church was the important thing and that it actually made up for the sin in my life. It was all a delusion. I recall in a men's group one night thinking to myself, "It seems like a lot of these guys really struggle and I seem to be doing alright." I had convinced myself that maintaining a good reputation was so important that I dare not bring my secret life into the open. Little did I know that the very reputation I was trying to protect was actually keeping me buried in sin and separated from God.

It wasn't until my mid-twenties that God really began to convict me about the double life I was leading. One day, on the heels of several sexual encounters, I was faced with the difficult decision to come into the light for the first time with my pastor.

When I told him the truth about my secret life, it was as if my heart was being set free. I was finally exposing the dark poison of sin in my life, and in exchange, God was giving me His life. I didn't realize at the time that it was one of the most important things I could do to achieve real freedom from the bondage of sin. My confession meant the end of my double life. The reputation I had tried to protect was no longer something I needed to hide behind. God had broken in and given me a sight of the Cross which set me free from the sin and shame that had enslaved me.

In some ways it was a painful experience, but I'm so grateful I went through it because it was the first step into the godly life the Lord had for me. Now I am blessed with a rich quality of life that is no longer found in myself, but in Jesus Christ.

A Study in God's Word

There are two Greek terms translated as "life" in the NT. The first, *psuche*, describes the living existence of any creature. The other term is *zoe*, which describes spiritual vitality. This is the emanating force of God. It is both what He possesses and what constitutes His very being. He is the life force of the entire universe. This explains why those banished from His presence in judgment will not experience "eternal life."

01 Look up the following verses that contain the Greek term *zoe*. Considering what is said about this term above, explain how this understanding sheds new light on the verse.

📖 John 20:31

📖 Romans 4:17

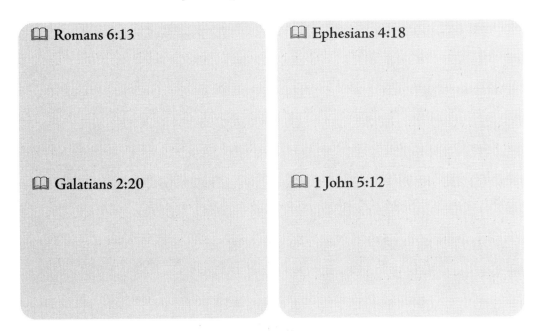

📖 Romans 6:13

📖 Ephesians 4:18

📖 Galatians 2:20

📖 1 John 5:12

Zoe is often connected to the word "eternal" (Greek, *aionias*). Most people who read "eternal life" in Scripture only think of duration—something along the lines of, "I'm a Christian and one day I'll inherit eternal life." At the very least this is a shallow view of this term. *Zoe* actually describes *quality* more than it describes *quantity*. A person who inherits *zoe* receives a life full of the very spiritual vitality that is inherent in God—and it begins in the here and now!

02 With that in mind, write out the following verses that reference *zoe*, but replace the words "life" or "eternal life" with the phrase "a life in God that is eternal in duration." The first one is provided as an example.

📖 Matthew 19:16b

Teacher, what good deed must I do to have **a life in God that is eternal in duration?**

📖 Matthew 7:14

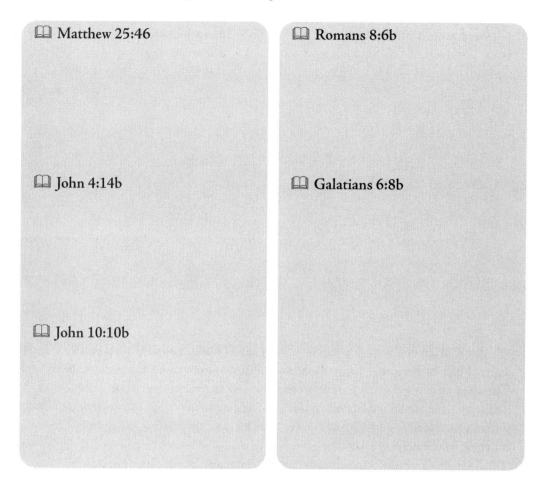

📖 Matthew 25:46

📖 Romans 8:6b

📖 John 4:14b

📖 Galatians 6:8b

📖 John 10:10b

Reflection Questions

01 Did changing the wording in the previous exercise give you a greater hunger for the real spiritual life that God is offering you? If so, how?

02 How has your selfishness robbed you from experiencing the rich quality of God's *zoe* in your daily life and relationship with others?

03 How would learning to live out God's love toward others increase your experience of the *zoe* of God?

04 If *zoe* is "a life in God that is eternal in duration," how do you think keeping your heart and mind focused on eternal things would affect your daily life?

Day Complete ✓

Day Twenty-Three
LIFESTYLE

Watch Truth #12:
You Must Repent of Sexual Sin

Sam's Story (Graduated 2021)

Christian activity was very important to me in my young adulthood. I thought that if I was going to church regularly, working full-time in ministry and was in a good relationship with my leaders, then I was obviously a Christian. But if a person were to observe my life outside of these things and, even worse, observe my inside world, then they would've known that I was actually far from God.

My life seemed to improve when I enrolled in secular college because I connected with a ministry that was available to foster fellowship between Christian students. The idea that I could actually grow closer to God in a secular setting was exciting to me. I even enjoyed a month of freedom from the pornography I had been regularly indulging in. Being able to experience real friendship with other Christians with nothing to hide was a real blessing to me.

However, my freedom proved to be short-lived and I eventually gave over again—something I kept to myself. My failure was devastating to me and just drained me of any resolve to keep fighting. I was still determined to remain involved with this Christian organization although I lost my enthusiasm for it.

I did eventually confess my secret sin to our small group leader, but by this time, I was becoming deeply enmeshed in a worldly lifestyle. I wasn't going to find freedom from sin until I experienced a real change in the way I was living my life.

If one looked past my church attendance, my leadership responsibilities, and my involvement in ministry, they would see a growing obsession with entertainment. In fact, instead of Jesus Christ being the focus of the fellowship I had with my Christian friends, the focus became the next blockbuster film. My infatuation with these movies led me to spend countless hours on YouTube watching movie critic videos. I'd also waste a lot of time viewing the most irreverent and irrelevant content, from perverse comedy to frivolous commentary on things that didn't matter. I didn't realize it at the time, but indulging in these different forms of amusement played a part in keeping me in bondage to sexual sin.

By the time I started working full-time for that Christian organization, I was habitually indulging in anything related to movies and YouTube commentary. I eventually switched out my smartphone for a basic phone and left my laptop at work, but to no avail as I would always find a way to get access to my favorite videos.

Needless to say, my lifestyle was dominated by entertainment by the time I applied to the Pure Life Ministries Residential Program. Looking back, I can see that my profession of faith was actually very hollow. It was pleasure that I lived for. Of course, everything changed at Pure Life and now the Lord truly has become the center of my life.

A Study in God's Word

A lifestyle could be described as the habitual conduct and pattern of living that defines a person's life. Perhaps the biblical figure whose lifestyle most resembles that of Americans would be Solomon's. He began with a sincere desire to walk with the Lord, but by indulging in one pleasure after another, he eventually became consumed with it. One need only read the book of Ecclesiastes he wrote toward the end of his life to see how miserable his hedonistic lifestyle left him.

The word "lifestyle" is not used in any of the more literal translations of the Bible. Instead, the biblical authors used the terms "walk" and "way" to describe what we would call a lifestyle. There is, however, an important distinction between the modern uses of these terms and how the Bible employs them. For instance, the term "lifestyle" in our day typically describes life in general terms whereas biblical writers always connected the terms "walk" and "way" to moral or spiritual issues.

01 Rewrite the following verses in your own words, finding a way to utilize the word "lifestyle" in your version.

📖 **Deuteronomy 10:12**

📖 **Micah 6:8**

📖 **Psalm 1:1**

📖 **2 Corinthians 5:7**

📖 **Psalm 81:12-13**

📖 **Galatians 5:16**

📖 **Jeremiah 6:16**

📖 **Ephesians 2:1-2**

📖 1 John 1:6-7

02 In light of these passages, describe in a succinct statement the manner of life you have lived thus far.

03 Now describe in about 250 words a lifestyle pleasing to God.

Reflection Questions

Every year, hundreds of men go through the Pure Life Ministries counseling programs. They come because their lives are plagued with selfishness, lust, pride and various destructive behaviors. But those who take the program seriously begin to find that they are being transformed.

01   What things have begun to change in your own life?

02   What are some of the things that still need to change so that your life is increasingly pleasing to God?

🕊 **Prayer Point**
Take some time to thank the Lord for the things that He has already begun to accomplish in your life. Then, express confidence that He will continue to work in you as you live in repentance. (Philippians 1:6)

Day Complete ✓

Day Twenty-Four

REPENT

Brian's Story (Graduated 2020)

I always had an understanding that viewing pornography was wrong, but I dealt with it the same way I dealt with any kind of sinful behavior: I put it in a "box." What I mean by that is that I learned to compartmentalize my life. For instance, when at high school football practice, I was in my football box and would talk and act like the other jocks. Later, when I had a job, I would be totally focused on work. It was the same dynamic at church or at home with my wife and two kids.

The most important compartment I maintained was my private box that no one was ever allowed into. That was the arena where my sexual sin flourished.

Now I did have a concept of right and wrong because I knew that things like lying, cheating, stealing, and other such actions were indeed wrong. But again, my life was sectioned off, and in my estimation, watching porn wasn't that bad. I wasn't *actually* cheating on my wife; I was just watching actors pretending to cheat on their spouses. I honestly didn't see anything in my life that needed to change. My family box was in good shape; same with my job box. The Christian compartment could be better, but God will sort that out, right?

The problem was, over time my sexual sin box began to spill over into the other boxes. For instance, my pornography fantasies resulted in flirty conversations with females which led to me having an affair. All the years of lying to keep the lines distinct in my mind had resulted in a separation from my wife and children. After twenty years of trying to keep my system going, I finally admitted that something should probably change. But my idea of change was to attend church more often and help the homeless people in our area. None of this changed who I was inwardly, though. It also didn't eliminate my regular involvement in pornography.

One day I confessed to my pastor that I had been with a prostitute. He knew that it was time to take more serious steps toward dealing with my problems. That's when I ended up at Pure Life Ministries.

Now the Lord began to work on my inward life. As God showed me through His Word how evil, dark and filthy my sin was, my perspectives about it began to change. But repentance wasn't simply turning away from sin; it also meant turning *toward* a person, Jesus Christ. For the first time in my life I began to see Him for who He really is. Coming to see the beauty of His purity and holiness caused me to hate my sin more than anything else.

It's been several years since that change occurred, and my life has continued moving further and further away from the person I once was. I can honestly say that now He has taken the center place in my heart. I am a changed man.

A Study in God's Word

Along with the many warnings in Scripture against indulgence in sexual sin, there are a couple specific NT examples that emphasize the need for repentance.

One such example is found in Revelation 2:20-22 where Jesus rebukes the leadership and congregation of Thyatira for tolerating Jezebel "who calls herself a prophetess and is teaching and seducing my servants to practice sexual immorality." Jesus goes on to say, "I gave her time to repent, but she refuses to repent of her sexual immorality."

Another instance of sexual sin among Christians is found in 1 Corinthians 5 where the apostle Paul also rebukes the congregation for tolerating it in their midst. He asks this carnal congregation, "Do you not know that a little leaven leavens the whole lump? Cleanse out the old leaven that you may be a new lump." (1 Corinthians 5:6b-7a ESV)

One of the primary functions of a pastor is to exercise church discipline when sexual sin is going on within a body. In this case, Paul instructed them, "When you are assembled in the name of the Lord Jesus and my spirit is present, with the power of our Lord Jesus, you are to deliver this man to Satan for the destruction of the flesh, so that his spirit may be saved in the day of the Lord." (1 Corinthians 5:4-5 ESV) This is important for the spiritual health of the congregation, but it is also important for the man who was living in open sin. The following commentary on this situation expresses the purpose behind it:

> A person who sins in this way needs to be placed among those who belong to the realm of darkness, even if he himself will ultimately be restored. His behavior is not fitting for "the kingdom of God" (4:20), and so he can have nothing to do with the Lord's people while he maintains his evil position… the purpose is restoration. The sense is that such people will once again "taste the other side," as it were, and so come to regret their actions and return in repentance and faith to the Lord.[i]

01   Explain this commentator's rationale on what is intended in the life of the man who has undergone the kind of church discipline Paul has instructed the Corinthians to implement.

02   Read 2 Corinthians 7:6-11 where Paul describes the repentance and restoration the Christians of Corinth experienced. Explain what you learn here about repentance, including the difference between "worldly sorrow" and "godly sorrow." Also describe the signs of true repentance that the Apostle mentioned.

Reflection Questions

01 Considering the content of the video and this study, explain what you think the difference is between making a resolution to quit sinful behavior and walking in a lifestyle of repentance.

02 Explain why you think that extreme measures (e.g., church discipline) are needed in the case of a person who will not repent of their sexual sin.

03 Based on what was shared in the video, explain how the Hebrew word for "turn" (Hebrew *shub*) and the Greek term for "repent" (Greek *metanoia*) work together to describe how a person leaves a lifestyle of sin and enters into a lifestyle of godliness.

04 Acts 3:19 promises that "times of refreshing" will follow true repentance. What does this tell you about what will happen in your heart and mind as you develop a lifestyle of turning away from your sexual sin?

05 Let's broaden the subject a little bit. Explain why repentance in every area of life should become the norm in a believer's life.

06 Discuss several other areas of your life where you would like to begin the process of transformation through repentance.

Day Complete ✓

Day Twenty-Five

WALKING IN THE FLESH

Watch Truth #13:
*Hedonism Opens the
Door for Pornography*

Jackson's Story (Graduated 2023)

There was a time when I constantly pursued one form of pleasure or another. There were occasions when I did genuinely want to have a better life in God, but I was unwilling to forsake the various pleasures that had become such a huge part of my life. At the top of this list was a growing addiction to internet porn. Not even powerful encounters with the Lord were enough to motivate me to change my ways.

I did have some sort of experience with the Lord when I was nineteen that stirred me to try to find freedom from pornography. The problem was that I wasn't taking the Word seriously and therefore gave little thought to Jesus' commands, such as my need to deny myself. When the Bible mentioned "walking in the flesh," I just thought it was describing an unpleasant person. I took the "lusts of the flesh" to be limited to sexual lust. I had these faulty understandings simply because I didn't put any effort into learning what the Bible actually taught.

At one point, I tried to quit viewing pornography but found that I had no internal strength to abstain from it. Then the Lord convicted me about my constant video gaming, so I managed to refrain for a brief period of time. But when boredom set in, I convinced myself that it was not sinful to "have some fun" or that "God wouldn't want me to be bored." Looking back, I can see that I was simply unwilling to give up my different pleasures. The truth is I believed that pleasure was the best part of life, so I made it the most important part of my life.

Any desire I had for the things of God was quickly crowded out by my love for entertainment and pleasure. Looking back on it now I can see that video gaming always paved the way into pornography. I was simply sowing to the flesh and would therefore reap more of the same. This unending cycle of fleshly fun leading to sexual sin killed off any meaningful desire I might occasionally feel for the things of God.

It was not until my situation became desperate that I saw I needed to act radically, and so I entered the Pure Life Residential Program. The drastic separation from the world I experienced there allowed me to sense the Lord drawing me to Himself. Now, for the first time in my life, I actually began to desire the things of God. My life was no longer consumed by time-wasting, meaningless activities. Those things that had been so important to me lost their appeal.

The Lord gave me new life and joy in Him, something the fleeting pleasures of sin couldn't offer. The shame, darkness, and defeat that had been my life before were replaced with a joyful, meaningful life. I have a real purpose in the kingdom of God and a new power to resist temptation which I never had before!

A Study in God's Word

A person who desires to overcome an addiction to pornography will eventually be forced to deal with the source of lust that is at work within him. At times the word "flesh" (Greek, *sarx*) refers to a person's physical body, but it is usually used metaphorically to describe a person's fallen nature or self-life.

✍ **Write out Romans 13:14.**

The flesh constantly craves satisfaction through food, comfort, pleasure, and yes, even pornography. It has no concern with obeying God. Many professing Christians have convinced themselves that so long as they believe what the Bible says about Christ, faithfully attend church services and identify themselves with Christianity that they are in good standing with God and on their way to heaven. However, Scripture tells a different story.

01 Read Galatians 5:19-21 and describe the outcome of living a life in the flesh.

02 Take a look at Romans 8:5-13 and list the six aspects Paul described of "walking in the flesh."

A   D

B   E

C   F

03 Now read these additional verses and share what else you learn about "walking in the flesh."

📖 Galatians 5:24

📖 Galatians 6:8

📖 Ephesians 2:1-3

📖 1 John 2:16-17

04 Paul offers a very simple explanation of how the believer should live his life. Read Galatians 5:16-17 and explain his formula for successful Christian living in your own words.

Reflection Questions

01 Today's study has helped you see very clearly that walking in the flesh is completely different from walking in the Spirit. In the table below, look at the various aspects of the fruit of the Spirit, and in the blank side of the table, write the opposite (e.g., next to love, write hatred).

Fruit of the Spirit	Fruit of the flesh
Love	
Joy	
Peace	
Patience	
Kindness	
Goodness	
Faithfulness	
Gentleness	
Self-control	

Perhaps you feel as if your life has come under a microscope the past few weeks, and you are discovering that there is more un-Christlikeness (or even sin) there than you ever realized before. Believe it or not, this is a good thing! As we draw near to God, the light of His holiness exposes the spiritual darkness that still exists in us.

02 What are some specific areas of your life where you now see you have been walking in the flesh? List out at least 4 examples.

03 In tomorrow's study we will be looking at walking in the Spirit. Why do you think that being able to see where you are "walking in the flesh" is a necessary precursor to learning to walk in the Spirit?

04 Perhaps today's study has revealed to you how greatly you need the Spirit's power and influence in your life. Spend some time meditating on Luke 11:9-13.

Day Complete ✓

Day Twenty-Six

WALKING IN THE SPIRIT

Jeremy's Story (Graduated 2011)

I came to the Pure Life Residential Program because my sexual sin was completely out of control. Over the course of three decades, I had experienced thousands of anonymous encounters with men. Upon arriving at Pure Life, I assumed if I could overcome my sexual sin that I could just go back to my old lifestyle—just without the illicit activity. I hadn't been there long, however, before I came into the reality that sexual sin was just a tiny part of a much larger problem—me, I was the problem!

I loved everything and anything that the world had to offer ME and I drank deeply from the cup of the world to please myself. I especially loved entertainment in all its forms—movies, YouTube, social media, binge-watching TV shows, ESPN, NHL, NFL, MLB. I loved Disney World, which offered the ultimate escape into a fantasy life where everything and everyone was wonderful. I loved going out to party—chatting with people with a beer or cocktail in my hand. God used my sexual sin to get me to a place where I could see the bigger problem of a life completely given over to a worldly, pleasure-driven mindset which was all focused around the idol of self.

The world as I knew it came crashing down about halfway through my time in the Residential Program. I can only say that a powerful sense of conviction from the Holy Spirit came over me after a counseling session. In an instant, I saw my life as it really was, with ME at the center of it all. I saw how my entertainment, pleasure-driven lifestyle had led to broken relationships, isolation, lost jobs, extreme debt. I was morally bankrupt—all because I allowed my lust for pleasure to rule my life. The reality of that revelation devastated me. In that moment, I came to a place of brokenness which led me into deep repentance. It was then that I came into a true relationship with the Lord.

That was only the beginning of a new life in Christ, though. How was I to go from being a total pleasure seeker to sincerely following God? It wasn't easy. Isaiah 55:6 says, "Seek the Lord while He may be found; call upon Him while He is near." I came to see that I couldn't do anything in my own strength. I needed His power in my life. I needed to keep seeking the Lord daily and calling upon His name. I needed the Holy Spirit to guide me, grow me, transform me.

Isaiah 55:1 says, "Come, everyone who thirsts, come to the waters…" (ESV) The problem was that I just wasn't thirsty, and it wasn't something I could work up. So in my desperation I just kept asking the Holy Spirit to give me the hunger and thirst for more of Him. This is a prayer the Lord promises to answer. (Luke 11:9-13) He did answer me and continues to answer me— He pours His Spirit out on me like living water that quenches my thirsty soul!

I am now a new creation in Christ by the redeeming power of His blood and the continuing work of the indwelling Holy Spirit.

A Study in God's Word

Galatians 5:16 tells us that if we, "walk in the Spirit," we will "not fulfill the lust of the flesh." So learning how to appropriate the power of the Holy Spirit in our daily walk is the key to living a life of victory over sexual sin—or any other lust arising from our flesh nature. Your self-life will gradually wither and die as you learn to live and walk in the Spirit. Where self has held dominion, now the Holy Spirit will reign in you.

Scripture indicates that when a person is born-again, he or she receives the Holy Spirit. Yet we also see the admonition in Scripture to continue seeking the Lord for His Spirit. (Luke 11:9-13) And it's been my experience that we can have however much of the Spirit that we desire.

01   Read Luke 11:9-13 and explain the sort of activity that would be involved with seeking the Lord for a greater infilling of His Spirit.

02 Consider 1 Corinthians 3:16-17 and explain what you think the apostle Paul meant by what he wrote. How would this correlate with your life?

03 Now read 2 Corinthians 3:17 and explain what role you think the Holy Spirit would play in a believer's life who has become addicted to some vice.

04 In yesterday's study, we looked at some verses in Romans 8 regarding walking in the flesh. Read the following verses and briefly describe what effects walking in the Spirit should have on a believer's life.

📖 **Romans 8:5**

📖 **Romans 8:6**

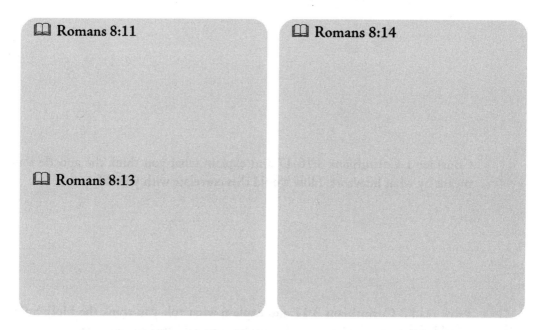

Romans 8:11

Romans 8:14

Romans 8:13

In Day 22, we looked at "the life of God" and the effects that life should have on a believer. In John 6:63, Jesus said, "It is the Spirit who gives life (Greek, *zoe*)..." Jesus is saying that the spiritual life should be a vibrant life in God, one full of love, joy and, well, life! And in John 7:38-39, Jesus said that anyone who believes in Him would receive the Holy Spirit, and "from his innermost being will flow rivers of living water."

05 Read the following verses where water is used as a metaphor for having the life of God. Briefly explain what you learn from each verse.

John 4:13-14

Isaiah 44:3

📖 Isaiah 55:1

📖 Isaiah 58:11

06 Now read Jeremiah 2:13 and explain what you think the Lord was referring to. How does viewing pornography fit into this picture?

Reflection Questions

01 Scripture refers to quenching the Spirit (1 Thessalonians 5:19), grieving the Holy Spirit (Ephesians 4:30) and resisting the Holy Spirit (Acts 7:51). Explain how it must affect the Holy Spirit when a believer views pornography. Dig deep here. Really consider the terms mentioned (grieving, quenching, resisting) as you answer this question.

02   In John 4:24 Jesus says, "God is Spirit, and those who worship Him must worship in spirit and truth." It has been my experience that much of the "worship" in today's church culture might be better termed "fleshly and fake." Think about what is going on inside you when you are singing hymns and choruses.

A   What does it mean for you to worship God "in Spirit?"

B   What does it mean to worship God "in truth?"

C   Why is it necessary to worship in both "Spirit and truth?"

03   Galatians 5:17 teaches us that the Spirit is opposed to the flesh, and the flesh is opposed to the Spirit. What would it look like for you to begin partnering with the Spirit in the war against your flesh?

☑ **Action Step**
Someone once said that many Christians expect God to give them million-dollar answers to their ten-cent prayers. Have you ever diligently and earnestly sought the Lord for the kind of life in the Spirit that you've read about today? If not, what can you do today to begin?

Day Complete ✓

Day Twenty-Seven

HEARING THE WORD

Watch Truth #14:
*Scripture Will Restructure
a Pornographic Mindset*

Ethan's Story (Graduated 2020)

Growing up, whenever I would hear the story of Mary and Martha, I always sympathized with Martha. As far as I was concerned, she got a bad rap. I mean if everyone just "lazed around" listening to Jesus, how would anything get done? It was clear to me that the church needs those who are hard at work taking care of others. Martha, in my opinion, was practical and someone who could be emulated.

So I embraced a busy lifestyle and justified it because it was for "ministry." But being busy about the Lord's business without stopping to listen to the Lord left me dry, cynical, and burnt out. This led me to seek pleasure from all kinds of sin and perversion, in spite of the fact that I was in the ministry.

I should have been listening to the Lord with the intent of obeying. The problem was that I couldn't bring myself to sit still long enough to hear Him.

When I finally came to the place where I wanted to be done with sexual sin, my mentor told me to make spending time with the Lord a priority. So the "too-busy-to-sit" guy (who had been silently judging all the lazy Marys) became determined to sit at the feet of Jesus until he knew he could hear His voice. My mind was still a cesspool of images, fantasies, and perverse desires, but that's where Jesus met me.

When I finally did learn to slow down, listen to and spend time with Jesus, something wonderful happened in my life. As I studied His Word, with the definite intention of hearing and obeying, I was blessed to receive a revelation about the character of God. As I came into a greater understanding of what the Lord is like, I sensed Him calling me to emulate the life that Jesus modeled for us. This was a call I wanted to respond to.

In my previous life of ministry, I was always striving, doing, and yes obeying, but my obedience was confined to a way of life that suited me. Since the Lord met me and changed my perspectives, a wonderful restoration of my heart and life has occurred. It wasn't a one-time "Aha!" moment, but as I kept looking to the Lord, listening to His voice, and heeding His commandments, He established me in a righteousness I never could have known apart from Him.

There's an old hymn called, "Sitting at the Feet of Jesus." One of the most poignant lyrics in that hymn, a line that still brings tears to my eyes, says, "For His love has been so gracious, it has won my heart at last."

Today, I'm a recovering Martha and still learning how to be a Mary—meaning, I'm still learning how to choose the "better thing." But that one thing—sitting at His feet and listening to His voice—has won my heart. It has transformed my mind, and it has sanctified my service.

A Study in God's Word

One of the unfortunate characteristics of many professing Christians has been the unhappy tendency to listen to and even enjoy a God-inspired message and then to walk out of the church building without the slightest intention of actually putting into practice the principles that were just communicated by the pastor. This propensity to hear without obeying the Word has been a tragic part of God's dealings with man from the beginning.

01   Read Ezekiel 33:30-32 and explain the situation the prophet was dealing with.

The word for "hear" in Ezekiel 33:32 is *shama*, which, in everyday language simply meant "to listen" or "to hear." However, the word took on a much stronger sense when it was God speaking through a prophet. The Jewish people of that day would have defined *shama* as "listening reverently with the intention of obeying."

Let's explore what our response to God's Word should be by examining how *shama* was used in some Old Testament Scriptures. In Deuteronomy 6:4 we find the most famous occurrence of this Hebraic term: "*Shema Yisrael, Yahweh Eloheinu, Adonai echad.*" ("Hear O Israel, Yahweh is our God, the Lord is One.")[1] This is the opening statement of the great *Shema*, the creed of Judaism that has played such an integral role in the Jewish faith over the centuries. No human could give it greater honor than Jesus Himself when He claimed it contained the greatest of all of the commandments.

02   Now read Mark 12:29-31. Break this passage down in detail and explain what it should mean to every believer.

---

1   Written as Moses said it, but the Jews later replaced God's name (*Yahweh*) with "the Lord" (*Adonai*) and most Bible translations adopted that change. "*Shema*" is a derivative of "*shama*."

03 Deuteronomy 11:26-28 contains the word *shama* twice. Depending on the version of your Bible it will probably be translated as either "listen" or "obey," because, as we noted above, it actually means both. Write this passage out, but each time you come to the term *shama*, replace it with this phrase: "listen reverently with the intention of obeying."

04 In Israel's history, there are numerous examples of how this promise from God was fulfilled, both His promise to bless and His promise to curse.

A   Read Genesis 26:4-5 and explain how *listening reverently with the intention of obeying* is demonstrated in this passage.

B   Read Exodus 5:2 and explain how *listening reverently with the intention of obeying* is not reflected in this passage.

Reflection Questions

01 This would be a good opportunity to consider how you've responded to sermons in the past. Have you been a "buffet Christian," picking out a few morsels that you can swallow, or have you been an earnest listener who intently tries to discern what God may be saying to you?

A How does being a buffet Christian impact a person's life spiritually?

B How does being an earnest listener contribute to spiritual growth?

C Can you think of a time that you acted upon something that you heard in a sermon and saw good spiritual fruit come from your obedience? Explain.

James 1:21 says, "Therefore putting aside all filthiness and all that remains of wickedness, in humility receive the word implanted, which is able to save your souls." One of the purposes of this study journal is to help you obey this command to "[put] aside all filthiness and all that remains of wickedness."

02   Where would you say you are at with making a genuine commitment to obey the Word in this way?

03   Why do you think humility is required to hear and obey God's Word? What could you do today to cultivate that kind of humility?

Day Complete ✓

Day Twenty-Eight

RESTORATION

Ben's Story (Graduated 2020)

I grew up in the nurturing environment of love and security typically found in a good Christian home. Yet, in my early teens I discovered sexual sin, which ripped open and completely wreaked havoc upon what had been a wholesome life. Within a short time, all natural joy vanished from my life, leaving me in isolation and oppressive darkness. I was plagued with the tormenting thoughts of unworthiness and never measuring up to God's standards.

To regain a sense of acceptance, I dove headlong into a worldly pursuit of academic knowledge and succeeded in becoming the valedictorian of my class. This opened the door to achieve the status and financial prosperity of a very successful career. Yet, the intensity of that demanding lifestyle exacted a hefty price. Neglecting family, abandoning close friendships, and stepping on other people were all justified means to achieving my goals.

Throughout this whole time I continued viewing pornography—sometimes for hours every night. I added binging on food to my carnal lifestyle, which led to excessive weight gain.

I eventually got married, but within two years my wife separated from me as she came face to face with my selfishness. This was devastating to me, and I responded by isolating myself in a friend's bedroom. For five days I did not contact anyone but wholly gave myself over to gluttony and pornography. At this point my out-of-control desires extended into my hard-earned career as I would spend upwards of eight hours of my workday viewing pornography. Unquestionably, I was facing the reality that divorce and being fired from my job was about to vanquish the dreams I once entertained of a happy and successful life. With nothing else to lose, I entered the Pure Life Residential Program.

The concept of turning to God in a real way was first brought to my attention by my counselor at Pure Life. He gave me the homework assignment to worship God at least fifteen minutes every afternoon for one month. At first, I was dumbfounded, not sure how to do this. Nevertheless, I did my best to obey his directive by simply presenting myself to God. I would utter a mechanical prayer such as, "God, here I am. I am not looking anywhere else, other than to You. I declare that You are worthy, holy, and full of love as Your Word says. Please help me."

The first two weeks of this discipline were very dry; yet I did not relent. As the days went by, I felt God's restoring power starting to work inside me. Joy, happiness, and delight were resurfacing in my life. I knew those emotions did not come from within myself; they were part of God's restoration of my life. By the time I reached the twenty-fifth day, I was actually looking forward to those afternoon times of worshiping the Lord.

By maintaining the daily discipline of turning to God for satisfaction, the bondage of sexual sin was eventually broken in my life. Today I still face the daily struggles of life. Yet, I am no longer suffering the torment that came from sexual fantasy, self-pity, and depression. The Lord has truly proven Himself to be a faithful restorer of my broken soul.

A Study in God's Word

In the OT, the Hebrew term *shub* is used to describe repentance some 1,300 times. However, it is also used with the idea of restoration. If you have been addicted to pornography, your soul has been polluted, tainted and marred by its wicked images. The wonderful news is that one of God's great passions is the restoration of damaged souls.

✎ Write out and memorize Psalm 23:3.

01 Job 22:23 provides one of the great conditional promises of Scripture: "If you return to the Almighty, you will be restored…" Explain what you think this statement means, especially in light of any pornography usage that has been in your life.

In the NASB, the English word "restore" is used some 125 times in the OT. In nearly all of these occasions, it is a translation of *shub*. However, there are occasions when *shub* is used to describe both repentance and restoration. For instance, in Jeremiah 15:19, the Lord says to His people, "If you return (*shub*), then I will restore (*shub*) you…"

02 Read Psalm 60:1. Can you relate to how David felt when he penned these words? Describe a time when you felt rejected by the Lord and what brought it about.

03 Read Psalm 19:7 and explain how spending time in God's Word consistently can make it possible for the Holy Spirit to do a deep work in your inward life.

04 The Word of God has the inherent power to restore the damaged soul. Read the following biblical statements regarding God's Word and briefly describe how it can restore a person who will truly "hear" and "obey."

📖 Matthew 4:4

📖 Matthew 7:24

📖 Matthew 13:23

📖 John 6:63

📖 John 8:31

📖 Romans 10:17

Reflection Questions

Hopefully, as you have read and meditated on the Word in today's study, it has given you hope that God can restore your soul, no matter how far you've gone down the path of sin and destruction. With that in mind, answer the following questions.

01 If you've been taking this study journal seriously, then whether you realize it or not, you've been spending time in God's Word regularly and practicing daily repentance. These are exactly the kinds of things that put us in a spiritual position to be restored by God's power! What kind of spiritual benefits have you experienced in your thoughts, attitudes and behaviors so far?

02 Perhaps you are very familiar with the feelings of hopelessness that often come with an addiction to pornography. Are you beginning to see the hope of restoration in your life? Explain your answer.

☑ **Action Step**

Listed below are three verses that are intended to encourage you to continue on the pathway of restoration. It would be a good idea for you to write one of them on a notecard and meditate on it throughout the day.

"If My people who are called by My name will humble themselves, and pray and seek My face, and turn from their wicked ways, then I will hear from heaven, and will forgive their sin and heal their land."
2 Chronicles 7:14 (NKJV)

"Come, and let us return to the Lord; for He has torn, but He will heal us; He has stricken, but He will bind us up."
Hosea 6:1 (NKJV)

"Repent therefore and be converted, that your sins may be blotted out, so that times of refreshing may come from the presence of the Lord."
Acts 3:19 (NKJV)

Day Complete ✓

Day Twenty-Nine

THE PRESENCE OF GOD

Watch Truth #15:
*To Overcome Temptation
You Must Have a
Prayer Life*

Caden's Story (Graduated 2020)

There was a time when my life was enveloped in a dark and oppressive atmosphere. This came about through a daily binge in pornography. The enemy used it to drag me down into a deep, dark pit. It happened so subtly that I didn't even realize it. It wasn't until I came to Pure Life and began to experience the presence of the Lord that I saw the reality of what I had given myself over to.

Other than fulfilling the obligatory work, church and social commitments, my life had spiraled down to spending all my time watching movies and viewing porn. Although I made every effort to portray the image of someone who was a sincere, dedicated Christ-follower, the truth was

that I never spent time seeking the Lord. It was all a façade.

Eventually I became so miserable that I began taking steps toward finding help, which is how I ended up in the Pure Life Residential Program. I remember in the very first chapel service being overwhelmed by the love of God. This first taste of God's presence impacted me deeply and set me on a path to find out how to live in that reality.

Initially, spending time in prayer was very difficult. I had never experienced a consistent prayer life in the past so establishing this discipline was a hard-fought battle. Over time though, I began to see things change in the way I thought, how I viewed other people, and most importantly how I saw God. I began to see the Lord as close and personal; someone who cared about my every need, no matter how small.

Experiencing the tangible presence of God was becoming a normal part of my life. There were times when words ended, and I could only weep as His love and mercy overwhelmed me. Praying for others became something I did because I truly cared for them and not simply because it was the right thing to do. Spending time in God's presence brought me out of the dark, oppressive atmosphere I had once endured, into one of freedom and life. Dark lustful thoughts were replaced with thoughts of God, His Word, and ways to please Him and bless others.

I have come to look forward to my prayer time because it has brought me into a place of closeness with God. It isn't always easy and at times I pray simply because I love God, not necessarily because I "feel" like it. But I still cherish those intimate times when He is very near and His presence is sweet. It is the reality of tasting and experiencing the goodness of God that has made porn become something I no longer desire. I've discovered something far better! I can truly say with David that there is only one thing I desire and that is to dwell in God's presence and gaze at His beauty. (Psalm 27:4)

A Study in God's Word

There is a Hebrew term *paniym* that is used over 1,700 times in the OT. When it comes to the Lord, it is typically translated either as "face," "presence" or "before" (e.g., "before the Lord.") And when you think about it, they all refer to being in close proximity to God.

01   Look up Psalm 27:4 and explain David's heart for God.

02   Now look at verse eight. One of the prevailing themes throughout Scripture is a call for God's people to seek His presence. Write out Psalm 27:8, replacing the word "face" with "presence."

03 Read Psalm 16:11 and explain what God's presence will do for the person who will seek it.

04 In James 4, we read, "Resist the devil, and he will flee from you. Draw near to God, and he will draw near to you." (James 4:7b-8a ESV) Explain the spiritual dynamic involved here and how it lays the foundation for overcoming a habit of viewing pornography.

When Moses was on Mount Sinai the Israelites made a golden calf and engaged in a disgusting, lascivious party. After all the Lord had done to free them from Egyptian bondage and to care for their needs in the wilderness, they continued to show by their actions that their hearts were still in Egypt. At this point the Lord told Moses, "Go up to a land flowing with milk and honey; but I will not go up among you, lest I consume you on the way, for you are a stiff-necked people." (Exodus 33:3 ESV) But when the people heard this "they mourned."

05 Look up Exodus 33:15 to see how Moses responded to the Lord. Write out a prayer, asking the Lord to give you this same heart.

Reflection Questions

Have you ever noticed that there is a huge difference between the mood at a football game and the mood at a prayer meeting? Between the way people act at a mall and at a worship service? Between the way you feel when you read your Bible versus when you're on social media?

The difference is that the enemy uses football games, malls and social media (among other things) to create carnal, ungodly atmospheres that encourage people to give over to the flesh and to sin. While the Lord uses things like prayer meetings, worship services and Bible reading to create spiritual atmospheres that can create a greater hunger for godly living. Can you see how important it is to carefully consider what kind of atmospheres you are subjecting yourself to?

01   When we seek God, we are seeking His presence, and the atmosphere that comes when the Lord shows up can have a powerful influence on a person's life.

A   Has there ever been a point in your life where you were diligently seeking the Lord's presence? What effect did this have on your thinking at the time?

B   What activities do you need to remove from or add to your daily routine to make more provision for the Lord's presence in your life?

02 Read Galatians 5:16-17 and describe how spending time in God's presence every morning would help prepare you for the temptations you might encounter that day.

03 Read John 14:21 and explain how Jesus "manifesting" Himself to you through His presence would help you in your battles with sexual temptation.

04 As we noted above, one of Satan's primary tactics in the 21st century is to use everyday things to establish atmospheres that are conducive to carnal living. Look at the list below. How do these ordinary activities affect the quality of your inward life?

A Social media and television

B News

C   Sporting events

D   Online shopping and malls

05   It's also true that certain places are unavoidable, despite the fact that the atmosphere in those places may be less than godly. Look at the list below. What could you do to maintain a godly atmosphere in your heart when you are in these places?

A   Work or school

B   Various stores

C   Homes of relatives or acquaintances

Day Complete ✓

Day Thirty

ESTABLISHING A PRAYER LIFE

Aidan's Story (Graduated 2021)

If you had been a fly on the wall of my life when I was twenty-years-old, you would have wondered if there were any reason at all to believe that I loved Jesus. Three years after my "profession" of faith, my relationship with the Lord was in shambles. I was watching porn multiple times a week and engaging in sexual immorality with others. The question that would have immediately come to your mind would have been, "What happened?!"

Other than an occasional journal entry or a quick "pop-up" prayer, I had not put forth any meaningful effort to cultivate a life of intimacy with Jesus. There was a certain sincerity to know the Lord, but I was content with outward displays of religion. As long as I seemed to be godly to others, I thought I was doing okay. Eventually, however, I gave up all pretext of following Him.

The kind of man God describes in Jeremiah 17:5-6 is a good description of my life at that time: "Cursed is the man who trusts in mankind and makes flesh his strength, and whose heart turns away from the Lord. For he will be like a bush in the desert and will not see when prosperity comes, but will live in stony wastes in the wilderness, a land of salt without inhabitant."

I remember often feeling devastated when others rejected me, but I cared very little about the Lord's opinion of my life.

My relationship with Jesus had gradually become nonexistent. Prayerlessness led to unbelief; unbelief led to sin; sin caused my life to spiral out of control. A barren desert is a good description of the emptiness of my life.

When I finally did come to the end of myself, the Lord immediately began calling me to Himself. Choosing to ignore my need for a consistent prayer life was simply no longer an option. If I was going to walk with Jesus, I couldn't just know about Him, I needed to know Him personally and intimately. This was only going to happen through a consistent time each morning in the Word and prayer. The Scriptures provided the opportunity to know about His character, but it was in prayer that I experienced His character—especially how loving and gracious He is—for myself.

As my prayer time with the Lord became an established practice, I began experiencing joy and peace that I had never known before. There was a freshness to this new walk with the Lord. I came to cherish my times with Jesus. His presence became a reality in my life. This kind of intimacy was something I had wanted for years… and now it was my daily experience!

Now, all these years later, I still enjoy intimacy with Jesus. He has sustained my prayer life and kept me anchored in Himself. I also find myself spontaneously thanking Him and singing songs of worship as I think of Him. The joy He imparts to my spirit has deepened and become a rock-solid foundation which I draw from as I minister to other men who are coming out of sexual sin.

Jeremiah contrasted the empty life of the wicked (mentioned above) with that of the godly when he wrote: "Blessed is the man who trusts in the Lord and whose trust is the Lord. For he will be like a tree planted by the water, that extends its roots by a stream and will not fear when the heat comes; but its leaves will be green, and it will not be anxious in a year of drought nor cease to yield fruit." (Jeremiah 17:7-8) I am so grateful to experience the fulfillment of this truth in my life.

A Study in God's Word

There is nothing that can affect a person's life for the good like the presence of God! If only people could know what it is like to be in His presence—to "taste and see that the Lord is good." (Psalm 34:8) So why is it that so few ever experience Him like this? The short answer is that most people are taken up with temporal things that please their lower nature and just don't take the time to cultivate a relationship with God. This is most unfortunate for those addicted to pornography because "where the Spirit of the

Lord is, there is freedom." (2 Corinthians 3:17 ESV) If there is one thing such people need it is the presence of God!

The Lord greatly desires to be in relationship with people. In fact, that one desire is the underlying reason this entire universe was created. God wants to be with *you*. Attending church services is part of that dynamic, but an intimate relationship comes through spending personal time with someone. In this case, it is established through a consistent, vibrant devotional life.

01 This desire of God is expressed beautifully in Jeremiah 29:11-13.[1] Read this passage and explain what you learn—especially regarding His feelings toward you.

02 Another passage that is beneficial is 1 Chronicles 16:8-12 which lays out the sort of activities that can be found in a robust devotional life. List out seven things included there that you could incorporate into your prayer life.

A

E

B

F

C

G

D

---

1   The primary context here is for the Jewish people who the Lord will redeem one day. However, it also expresses His desire for any human—whether Gentile or Jew.

03   In the OT, establishing this vital connection to the Lord is portrayed in the idea of seeking His presence. Look up the following verses and explain in your own words what you learn.

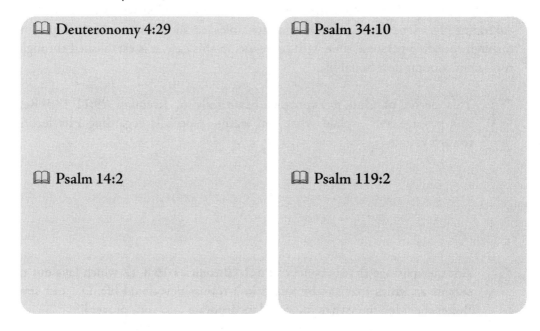

📖 Deuteronomy 4:29

📖 Psalm 34:10

📖 Psalm 14:2

📖 Psalm 119:2

Reflection Questions

Experience has repeatedly confirmed that the only way for someone to enjoy an effective prayer life is for them to make it an established habit in their daily life. In other words, the person must commit to spending time in prayer at the same basic time every day. Those who allow sleepiness, distractions or simply not "feeling" like praying will become inconsistent with it and inconsistency will prove to be the death of a vibrant devotional time.

Let's put it in terms of someone who decides to quit smoking. So one morning he throws his cigarettes away, but on the third day he wavers and smokes a cigarette. Had he stuck with it, in two weeks he would have been pretty much free of it. Now he must begin the whole process all over again.

Starting any new habit (that isn't gratifying to the flesh) can be difficult to get going, but once a habit has become established, it becomes much easier. Humans have the capacity to form godly habits that can result in a godly lifestyle. A daily prayer time is arguably the most important habit a believer can establish. If he will stick with it, it won't be long before it is second nature to him.

At the Second Check-In, you were encouraged to make a commitment to establish a daily prayer life for at least ten minutes every day. Let's review the essential aspects of a vibrant prayer time and see how you've been doing:

01 Decide *when* you will pray. Remember we said the best time in every day is before the hustle and bustle begins.

A. What time do you meet with the Lord for your prayer time each day?

B. Have you been consistently waking up early enough to have uninterrupted quality time with the Lord?

02 Decide *where* you will pray. You were advised to find a place in your house or dorm that lends itself to having quality time with God.

A. What place have you settled on for your prayer time each day?

B. Have you experimented with walking while you pray, or journaling or typing your prayers? What were the results?

03 Determine *what* you will pray about. The acrostic ACTS (Adoration, Confession, Thanksgiving, Supplication) was offered as an example of one prayer method you could use. Another option was making a list of various groups of people to pray for (church, family, coworkers, classmates, etc.) on different days of the week. And of course you should be praying for your own spiritual needs.

A   Describe the method or format you use for your daily prayer times.

B   What are the personal spiritual needs you've been praying for?

04   Lastly, we addressed the option of having someone help keep you accountable with your commitment. How did that work out for you?

If you have not yet established a consistent prayer life, accountability is no longer simply an option—it's time to find someone who will be able to help keep you accountable. Describe your plan and timeframe for establishing the accountability you need. Remember, establishing a spiritual discipline like this can be difficult, so be prepared to fight for it!

> ☑ **Action Step**
> Has your prayer time lengthened from the ten minutes you started with? If not, I want to encourage you to start building up your daily time until you have a regular habit of spending at least 30 minutes in prayer each morning.

05   Have you seen any answers to your prayers? Describe some notable examples.

Day Complete ✓

☑ THIRD CHECK-IN

My hope is that at this point you are beginning to see some real changes taking place in your spiritual battle. Again, the most important thing to look for is internal change. What I mean is that instead of feeling utterly hopeless that you can ever get free of your addiction to pornography, you should be starting to see light at the end of the tunnel.

Over the past few days you have been considering the necessity of having a consistent time with the Lord every morning. I can't stress strongly enough how important this is! I can look back to the beginning of 1985—when I began having a time with God every morning—and see that this was the turning point in my life. If you haven't already, I hope you will get that new habit established right away. It's the very thing you've been needing!

Let's look at the commitments you should have implemented from the First and Second Check-Ins.

- ☑ I have been doing this study every day.
- ☑ I have cut off all avenues to pornography.
- ☑ I have told my spiritual leader about my secret life.
- ☑ I have established a consistent prayer life.
- ☑ I have started a gratitude journal.
- ☑ I have implemented my plan to have regular fellowship with my wife or other believers.

Now, let's add some new commitments.

☐ **I will not watch any ungodly entertainment (i.e. YouTube, television, streaming services).**

Any Christian who makes a determined decision to rid themselves of the evil of pornography should be commended, but what so many Christians do not realize is that the world's entertainment is often the very thing that keeps them so susceptible to sexual lust. Visual media that contains cursing, gratuitous violence or sensuality is just as much a part of the devil's kingdom as pornography is. If you really want freedom, you're going to have to take a stand against *all ungodly entertainment*.

☐ **I will eliminate easy access to any social media accounts that have been a consistent avenue of failure.**

Social media has the potential to be used for good in certain situations. But for those who have been addicted to pornography, having open access to platforms like Tik Tok, Instagram and Facebook often becomes a source of continual temptation and frequent failure. If you have ongoing struggles with any social media platforms, it's time to eliminate easy access. You might consider deleting any unnecessary social media accounts or giving someone else your password so that you can only check it when you are with them. Do whatever it takes!

☐ **I will make plans to continue my daily Bible time after this study ends.**

This study will end in just ten days, so it's time to decide what you will use to continue having a daily time in God's Word when you've finished. Here are some resources to consider.

1 *The Walk Series* from Pure Life Ministries. This series is designed to help you experience the victorious Christian life through a deeper life in God. Whether you prefer topical studies or going through a book of the Bible, each

volume of *The Walk Series* will show you how to keep
moving deeper and deeper into God's glorious kingdom.

2 *The New Inductive Study Series* by Precept Ministries. This series has
a separate study for every book of the Bible and offers an excellent
introduction to the Precept Bible Study Method. With guided questions
and 20-30 minutes of daily homework, these books are ideal for personal
study, one-on-one mentoring, small groups, and family devotions.

3 *Encounters with God* series by Henry Blackaby. This series has
a specific study for many books of the New Testament and
offers interpretations of the text, story illustrations, related
Bible verses, questions for reflection and life applications.

4 *Following God* series (various authors). These interactive Bible study
workbooks bring you into a closer walk with God as your Father
and Friend. There are three major types of studies: The Character
Series, The Discipleship Series, and the Through the Bible Series.

Day Thirty-One
THE NECESSITY OF TEMPTATION

Watch Truth #16:
Temptation is a Winnable Battle

Gordon's Story (Graduated 2007)

It has been over fifteen years since the Lord set me free from the bondage of pornography. When I compare who I am now with the man I was before, what stands out to me is the difference in how I deal with temptations. They have never completely gone away, but they have certainly lost their enticing luster.

There is a part of me that wishes I could boast of a life filled with ease and relaxation. In truth, it has been more like following Joshua into battle against the hordes of pagan enemies in the Promised Land! Even though I've complained at times about still having to face temptations, I know they are a necessary element in strengthening my faith.

When I was in the Residential Program, I ran across a passage that continues to encourage me because it helps me understand why I am still in the fight for purity. Prior to entering Canaan, God told His people, "I will not drive them [your enemies] out before you in a single year, that the land may not become desolate and the beasts of the field become too numerous for you. I will drive them out before you *little by little*, until you become fruitful and take possession of the land." (Exodus 23:29-30)

When I was addicted to pornography, I desperately wanted the Lord to "zap" me and completely set me free from its grip. But this passage in Exodus shows that emptying the land of enemies all at once would not have benefited God's people. Their adversaries were left in the land so that the Israelites would become experienced warriors who knew how to trust the Lord for the victory.

I know that the Great Antagonist of my soul is out there and that he has many cohorts. Twenty-first century American culture is rife with the enchanting voice of the seductress. So for me, *expecting* that temptations will come is half the battle. *Knowing* that the Lord is with me and for me is the other half.

Armies must be prepared to battle an enemy at a moment's notice. My preparation for battle comes through a daily quiet time, which has been one of the most crucial elements in walking in victory over pornography. And it must be more than just a fifteen-minute exercise. Making sure that this time is more relational than academic is key to having deep and meaningful Bible study, prayer, and fellowship with the Lord. Without having established this discipline, I believe I would have backslidden long ago. But because I'm continually in the Word and prayer, when temptations do come, I lean into the Lover of my soul instead of allowing them to carry me away.

A Study in God's Word

Temptation is anything that tests the reality and sincerity of a person's faith in Christ by alluring him or her into sin. Temptations can appear in countless forms and can appeal to a multitude of different human desires.

Whatever the specific temptation may be, you can be sure there are two things at work. On the one hand, the devil is making his appeal to your flesh nature with the intention that you will fall and give into sin. He relishes it when we gratify our desires at God's expense. But God is at work in the same situation, appealing to your spirit, with the desire that you would withstand the temptation, that you would endure it and emerge victoriously over it. God delights in seeing us hold faith and refuse to violate His standards by gratifying ourselves.

✍ **Rewrite 1 Corinthians 10:13 in your own words.**

In the field of intelligence (e.g., the CIA or British MI6), during a cadet's training, officers will put him in different situations to see how he will respond. On some occasions the trainee might be subjected to being arrested and mercilessly interrogated. At other times he might be flown into a wilderness area and told to find his way out. Still other times he could be approached by a beautiful seductress. The point of all these situations is to find out what he's made of; how deeply he's committed to the cause; what can be expected of him once he's operating in the world of espionage.

01   Look up the following verses and explain in your own words what you learn about how God deals with His children.

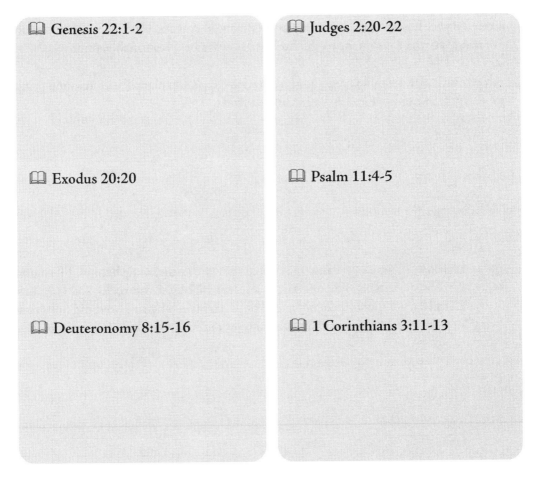

📖 **Genesis 22:1-2**

📖 **Judges 2:20-22**

📖 **Exodus 20:20**

📖 **Psalm 11:4-5**

📖 **Deuteronomy 8:15-16**

📖 **1 Corinthians 3:11-13**

📖 1 Peter 1:6-7

If you are just now starting to take your battle with temptation seriously, I want you to understand that it is perfectly normal to feel overwhelmed. You're not accustomed to battling temptations with the idea of never giving in. Don't despair! You can win this battle! The beginning stages of victory are the most difficult, but there is no way around them. It is something you must go through. You see, until you face this process of testing, your commitment to the Lord will always be questionable, unproven.

02 With that in mind, read 1 Timothy 3:8-10 and explain Paul's reasoning in his admonition to Timothy regarding deacons.

03 In Mark 4, Jesus explains to His disciples the meaning behind His famous *Parable of the Soils*. For our purposes, let's highlight the rocky soil specifically. Read Mark 4:5-6 as well as verses 16-17. Explain why this seed did not grow to bear fruit and how that can relate to temptations in the life of a young believer.

04 Read James 1:12 and explain what you learn about the final outcome of learning to obediently persevere through the trials of life.

Reflection Questions

01 Consider the metaphor used in the video about a boxer, and then read what Jesus said to His disciples in Matthew 26:41. How would you relate the boxer metaphor and Jesus' words to your life? Explain how you have failed to prepare yourself in the past and what you think you should do differently going forward in life.

02 Read 1 Corinthians 10:13 again. In the past, have you believed that winning the battle with sexual sin is impossible? How does believing that the battle is winnable help you go forward?

03   As mentioned above, people who enter the military intelligence field often go through a process of testing. Those who endure the period of testing come out the other side with a deeper loyalty to our country and a greater confidence in their ability to carry out the mission no matter how difficult it might be.

A   What spiritual qualities do you think will be added to your character as you begin to win those battles with temptations?

B   How might going through those daily temptations actually make you an asset for God's kingdom?

04   Have you enjoyed a time of freedom from viewing pornography? Can you see from all you've learned today how it could be a sign that you are getting close to putting this sin behind you for good?

Day Complete ✓

Day Thirty-Two

THE REASONS FOR TEMPTATIONS

Elijah's Story (Graduated 2013)

Although I grew up in the church, I knew that I hadn't been born-again. But I believed the day would come that it would happen. This was very hopeful because I had come to believe that all my struggles would come to an end and I would be filled with the love of God for everyone. Life would become incredibly easy as the Lord showered me with all sorts of gifts.

However, I came to realize that suffering, temptation, and trials are an integral part of the Christian life. After God saved me out of sexual sin, the temptation to give into lust was still very intense. When temptation came my first thought was usually, "How can I get out of this as quickly and easily as possible so I don't have to endure a painful battle"?

One day a vivid memory of a pornographic video I had seen came into my mind when I was in the shower. During past times of temptation, I would just ask the Lord to help me or I would redirect my mind. But in this particular instance, the temptation was too strong. I cried out to the Lord, and I was reminded of the story of Joseph, when he fled from Potiphar's wife. I knew I needed to flee so I quickly got out of the shower, put my clothes on, and went outside where I knew I would be in the presence of others.

The Lord has proven Himself faithful to me in my battles with temptation. As much as I wish that I didn't have to fight temptation, I can see how the Lord uses it in my life to teach me how to depend on Him instead of myself. Each time God brings me through one of these battles, I find my hatred for sin growing just a little bit more.

I am so thankful that the Lord has used these struggles to build character in me and make me more like His Son. Because I have experienced His faithfulness so many times in the past, I know that He will come through for me in the future. That gives me confidence when I find myself in the midst of a new battle.

If I must endure these battles during my stay on earth, so be it. I would rather be in the position to have to depend on God than to live with an attitude of self-sufficiency!

A Study in God's Word

Life in this world is full of opportunities to disobey God. The truth is that temptations to sin are a necessary part of the Christian life. So let's dig down a little bit deeper today as to why believers must face temptations and trials.

01 One of the positive aspects of temptations that come our way is that they provide opportunities to defeat the enemy. Matthew 4 describes the episode in the life of Jesus where He had to go into the wilderness to face Satan himself. Read Matthew 4:1 and explain why you think God put Jesus into this situation and how it relates to your own issues with pornography.

One other positive aspect of temptation is that it can break down our natural self-sufficiency, self-reliance and self-will—the very attitudes that lead us into sinful thinking and actions in the first place! By allowing us to be overwhelmed beyond our own strength and wisdom, He wants to teach us to turn to Him in the heat of the battle.

02 Read Proverbs 3:5 and explain how it relates to facing temptation.

03 Read 2 Corinthians 12:7-9 and explain any additional insights you learn from Paul's experience.

Yet another positive aspect of temptation is that it plays a role in developing a hatred for sin in a believer. God is not shortsighted. He is looking at the long-term goal of making His child more Christlike. In His great wisdom and providence, even failures can work for the good of those who are sincerely fighting. Each defeat deepens his hatred of the sin that has caused him and his loved ones so much suffering. As his hatred for that particular sin intensifies, his level of consecration to God deepens.

04 Read the following verses and explain what you learn.

📖 Psalm 26:5

📖 Psalm 36:1-2

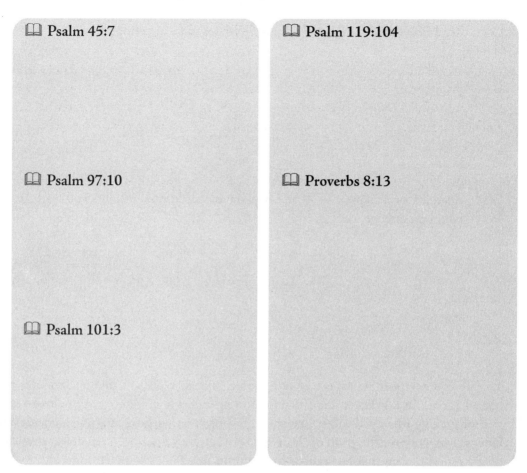

📖 Psalm 45:7

📖 Psalm 119:104

📖 Psalm 97:10

📖 Proverbs 8:13

📖 Psalm 101:3

05 Now perhaps the words that James wrote 2,000 years ago will make more sense. Read James 1:2-4 and, in light of the past two days' homework, explain what you think he was saying.

Reflection Questions

Consider the case of Peter during the Last Supper. Jesus had just shared His heart, warning the remaining disciples that they would all "fall away" before the events of the night were over. Read Peter's response in Matthew 26:33-35. His reaction here is a good example of untested Christians who naively think they have the spiritual maturity to withstand great temptation.

01 Explain any unwarranted confidence you've had in yourself in the past.

02 In 1 Corinthians 10:12, Paul told the Corinthian believers, "Let him who thinks he stands be careful that he doesn't fall." What wisdom does this verse give you in your battle against pornography?

03 Countless men have told us they would gladly rid themselves of all temptation
    if they could. How different is the apostle Peter's perspective on the benefit of
    testing and trials! (see 1 Peter 1:6-7)

  A How might Peter's own experience of falling into temptation
     (by denying Jesus) have given him the perspective that
     being tested and tried is actually a glorious thing?

  B How might the battles you are facing now produce that same perspective
     in you if you endure those temptations over the long haul?

Day Complete ✓

Day Thirty-Three

THE SPIRIT OF THE WORLD

Watch Truth #17:
*The Spirit of the World
Wants to Seduce You*

Jake's Story (Graduated 2021)

My dive into homosexuality began in an unlikely way. It started with a seemingly innocent desire for attention and affirmation from others. And if you would have told me when I was age twelve that seven years later I would be throwing off all semblance of Christianity and giving myself over to the gay lifestyle, I would have thought you were crazy. But that is exactly what happened, and here's how it came about.

Growing up in a conservative home, we had no television and didn't buy a computer until I reached adolescence. You would think this would have prevented me from indulging in the things of the world—and it did for a time. However, I also attended public school, where the kids around me weren't from upright Christian homes. Somewhere along the way a desire to fit in with my peers began to grow inside of me. I felt restricted by my boundaries and longed to have the same access to entertainment they enjoyed. I attempted to make friends with the "cool kids," but I always felt like I was outside of their inner circle. This left me craving deeper relationships with other boys.

My first sexual encounter happened when I was about ten. More encounters occurred during the following years. I bought an iPod touch when I was twelve and stumbled into the world of pornography. Very quickly the content I was viewing turned homosexual.

Over the next six years, I dove deeper into pornography, and at age nineteen I entered my first relationship with another man. I was in four different relationships during the next two-and-a-half years. Having been in church my whole life I knew homosexuality was sinful, but now I threw off all restraint and embraced the belief that God approved of my lifestyle. Spending many hours on social media and watching provocative movies led to weekends of indulgence in sexual sin. My desire to fit in had turned into the kind of full-blown life of sexual perversion that the world heartily endorses.

I was in sync with the spirit of the world and should have been happier than ever. But the gay lifestyle was making me increasingly miserable, empty and lonely. The more I pursued this worldly living, the more depressed I became.

I am eternally grateful the Lord did not allow me to continue further down this path of destruction. After this dark season of my life, God came to me, showing me how I had become enslaved to sin. He helped me to see that I was missing the love that truly satisfies—the love of Jesus Christ. And it was His love that melted my heart and brought me into true repentance. The spirit of the world had taken the throne of my heart, but now I was able to give it to the Lord.

This was only the beginning, though. He needed to train me how to renounce ungodliness and worldly passions, and to live a self-controlled, upright and godly life in this present age. (Titus 2:12) I have been free from the power of this dark world for several years now and can boldly declare that Jesus has set me free by His mercy and love.

A Study in God's Word

The concept of the necessity for believers to separate themselves from the influences of the world is as old as His dealings with Israel. When Moses led the Jewish people into the wilderness, he laid out some six hundred laws that were for the purpose of distinguishing them from the idolatrous pagan nations surrounding them.

01 As the people of Israel were about to enter the Promised Land, Moses gave a series of messages to them which became the Book of Deuteronomy. Read the following statements he made regarding idolatry and briefly explain what he said and what you think might be the purpose behind those statements.

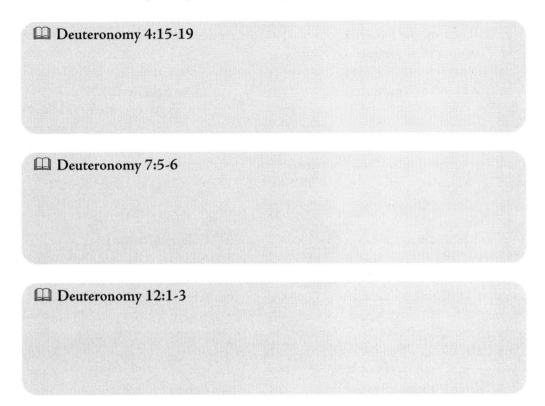

📖 **Deuteronomy 4:15-19**

📖 **Deuteronomy 7:5-6**

📖 **Deuteronomy 12:1-3**

02 Rewrite James 1:27 in your own words and explain what you think James was saying to his readers.

03 Look up the following verses about the world and briefly explain in your own words what you learn.

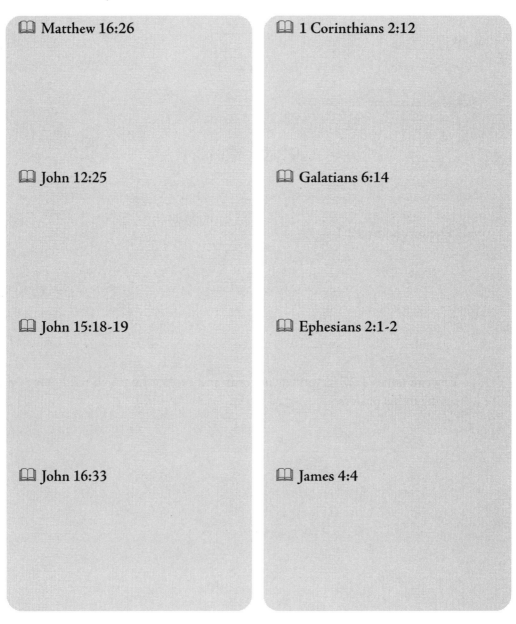

📖 Matthew 16:26

📖 John 12:25

📖 John 15:18-19

📖 John 16:33

📖 1 Corinthians 2:12

📖 Galatians 6:14

📖 Ephesians 2:1-2

📖 James 4:4

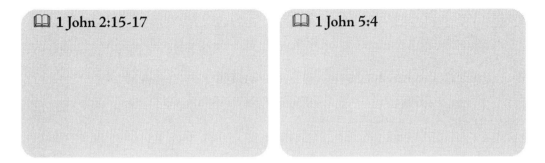

📖 1 John 2:15-17

📖 1 John 5:4

Reflection Questions

In today's study, we've clearly seen that God has always required His people to be holy, that is, to separate themselves from the ungodly influences of this world and to wholeheartedly worship and serve Him. And most Christians are willing to admit that pornography is a horribly evil influence that is inspired by the evil spirits of this world. What Christians have a much more difficult time coming to grips with is that the vast majority of what comes through our entertainment-obsessed culture is also inspired by these spirits.

01 Take a few minutes to recall your activities after work or school this past week.

A How much of your free time did you spend watching television, surfing the internet or interacting with social media?

B If you spend a significant amount of time weekly consuming media, it's highly likely that you are being engulfed in the "spirit of the world." What are some specific ways you can see how this constant influence has shaped your perspectives in an ungodly way?

C   Can you see how a regular fare of worldly entertainment
    would smooth the path into viewing pornography?

D   How might a constant flow of the world's entertainment be
    counteracting your efforts to draw closer to God through this study?

Even non-Christians have often expressed that "unplugging" from media has had a
positive effect on their lives. And in the video, you heard a testimony of how the true
influence of the spirit of this world could only be discerned after television had been
completely cut off.

02   Make a list of three concrete steps you could reasonably take to lessen the world's
     influence in your life.

A

B

C

Day Complete ✓

Day Thirty-Four

THE CALL

Cameron's Story (Graduated 2021)

I remember the words my counselor said to me very clearly one day: "You need to pray about coming to Kentucky." Those words forever changed my life.

During most of my early years I was given over to lust, fantasy and acting out sexually. I lived my life to entertain myself in any way that I could, and the main focus of this was sexual sin. While all of this was going on in secret, I also participated in church and was a leader in both high school and college. I was determined to maintain my image of being a nice guy who had it all together in life. The reality was that I had a secret life completely secluded from others that left me unhappy and hopeless.

All this misery was actually a blessing from the Lord, as it led me to seek help. I went to a mentor of mine at the time, and he recommended that I enroll in the Overcomers At-Home Program with Pure Life Ministries. It didn't take my counselor long to see that my issues were serious enough to need a more intense approach. I needed radical surgery: to completely cut myself off from the things I had been idolizing. The way out the Lord provided for me was a move to Kentucky.

This move was not just a slight change in lifestyle. I literally lost everything. I was fired from my job, quit coaching soccer, gave most of my things away and moved out of my apartment. The most difficult sacrifice I had to make was the relationship I was in. All of this was necessary for me to see how completely I had allowed the lust for things to control my life. I had so many distractions and hobbies that I had no room for God.

The most vital thing that the Lord was calling me to give up was the sense that I needed to be constantly entertained. My entire life revolved around consuming and indulging in various forms of entertainment.

Yes, sexual sin was the primary vehicle, but the Lord had to show me that selfishness was the deeper issue. I was willing to look at, watch or do almost anything in my pursuit of pleasure. He was calling me out of myself and into Himself; calling me to live selflessly; to be a blessing to others.

Over time, the Lord set me free of the constant desire to feast on entertainment. I am thankful for the call the Lord put on my life because it has forever changed my life.

A Study in God's Word

Abraham, the father of our faith, grew up in Mesopotamia. He was called to leave that region and go to what would one day be the Promised Land. That "call," in one form or another, has been issued to every believer since.

01   Read Genesis 12:1-5 and write out the 3 things God commanded Abraham to leave and how each of those might apply to God's people today.

A

B

C

✐ **Write out 1 Thessalonians 4:7.**

02 Read Romans 8:28 and explain the two prerequisites to the good that is promised.

A

B

03 The word "church" in the Greek is *ekklesia* which is derived from two Greek words: *ek* "out of" and *kletos* "called." It literally means "called out ones." Write out the following verses replacing the word "church" with the phrase, "called out ones."

📖 Acts 8:1

📖 Acts 9:31

📖 Acts 8:3

📖 Acts 12:5

📖 Acts 20:28

04 Read 2 Corinthians 6:14-7:1 and explain in your own words what you learn, especially as it pertains to viewing pornography.

Reflection Questions

01 In the 2 Corinthians passage you just read, Paul made it very clear that those who walk with God will be enabled to become increasingly more holy in their hearts and lives. However, many professing believers have incorrect views of holiness. Do any of the following statements reflect the way you have viewed holiness in the past? Circle the ones that apply.

1 I should live a holy life, but it's impossible.
2 Holiness would keep me from living a happy life.
3 Believing in Jesus is what makes me holy, not how I live my life.
4 I've never really thought seriously about holiness.

02 Think about the statements you circled above. How might the attitude represented in those statements hinder you from finding victory over pornography?

03 Based on your study of the word *ekklesia*, and God's call to His church, how do you think your spiritual life and influence is compromised by involvement with the world?

04 God's call to Abraham was a physical picture of the spiritual call that He issues to every true believer. What might it look like for a person to respond to that call in 21st century America?

Day Complete ✓

Day Thirty-Five
THE BATTLE

Watch Truth #18:
*Failure is not Defeat in Your
Battle with Sexual Sin*

Rob's Story (Graduated 2009)

If I had to describe the early days of my walk with Jesus using only one word, I would probably choose the word BATTLE. I remember so vividly feeling like *everything* was against me. It seemed like lust, criticism, self-pity, discouragement and pride dominated my thinking.

Looking back, it makes sense why the battle was so intense at the beginning. For years I had habituated myself to think and act in a selfish and sinful way. So, although I was on a totally new spiritual path, I still had to work out the new life that Jesus had provided for me.

Probably one of the most difficult battles I had to face was discouragement.

Looking back I think my problem was that I wanted the Christian life to be easy. One thing that was instilled in me during my time at Pure Life Ministries is that quitting is NOT an option.

To strengthen me in my personal struggles, I would memorize Scripture. For a long time my favorite verse was Psalm 9:9-10, which says "The Lord is a stronghold for the oppressed, a stronghold in times of trouble. And those who know Your name put their trust in You, for You, O Lord, have not forsaken those who seek You (ESV)."

Although the struggles were fierce at times, there were two different things that really helped me to keep fighting.

The first was that I hated the kind of life I had lived in the past. No matter how many failures I had with lust, selfishness or pride, returning to the life I had lived where I allowed sin to go unchecked was unthinkable. The second thing was that I had tasted of God's goodness. His life and love were so incredibly different than the darkness I had lived in for so long. The knowledge that He was offering Himself to *me* kept me pursuing Him with desperation.

Little by little, things began to change in my life. I was able to see light at the end of the tunnel. The sins that felt like they had had a stranglehold on my life were losing their grip on me.

If I were to describe how things changed in my life, I wouldn't be able to point to any particular big moments. What does stand out to me are the little steps of obedience and the fruit that eventually came from bringing my thoughts and actions into alignment with the Word of God. I remember sensing the sweetness of His presence during my morning times with Him. It seems as though there was a constant cry in my heart for His help and strength. There were also many occasions when I knew I was wrong about something and had to humble myself before Him. Through it all He was incredibly patient with me, encouraging me when I failed and disciplining me when I went astray.

If I could sum it all up, I would just say that even though the Christian life was intensely difficult at times, I don't regret the hardship of it one bit. How could I? That battle brought me into a true life in God!

A Study in God's Word

Certainly by now you realize that you are living your life in the middle of a battleground. What's worse, because of sin, you have probably gone deep into enemy territory, and you must now fight your way out. Don't fear! You can live the rest of your life in victory, but it will require a great deal of struggle—especially in the early days of this journey.

✍ Write out 1 Timothy 6:12.

The word "against" is used some 1,300 times in the Bible, and it is primarily used to describe conflict in one way or another. Unquestionably, the road to heaven goes through a great battlefield.

01 The following verses that contain the word "against" describe some of the great battles that occur in the unseen realm. Look up each reference and briefly explain what you learn about this warfare.

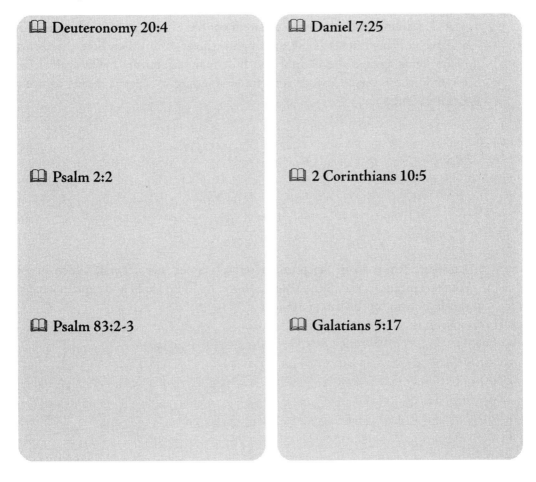

📖 Deuteronomy 20:4

📖 Daniel 7:25

📖 Psalm 2:2

📖 2 Corinthians 10:5

📖 Psalm 83:2-3

📖 Galatians 5:17

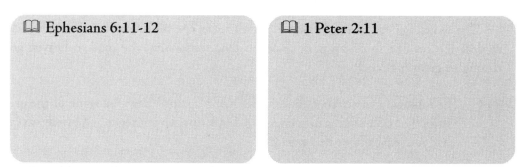

📖 Ephesians 6:11-12

📖 1 Peter 2:11

02 The verses above describe many different conflicts in the great war between God and Satan. This impacts how men fight against each other, how the spiritual realm fights against the natural and how man stubbornly fights against God. How do those verses impact your understanding of what it means to live the Christian life?

03 Another term used in Scripture is "strive" (Greek, *agonizomai*) which in most contexts means to "fervently struggle." Look up Luke 13:24 and explain what you think Jesus meant by this statement.

04 Yet another important NT term that is used to describe the battle we are in is "overcome" (Greek, *nikao*). Look up the following verses and apply each one to your battle with the temptation to return to pornography.

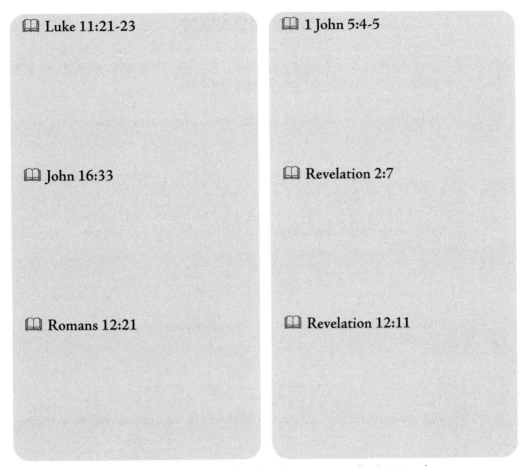

📖 Luke 11:21-23

📖 1 John 5:4-5

📖 John 16:33

📖 Revelation 2:7

📖 Romans 12:21

📖 Revelation 12:11

05 Someone said, "Success is not final. Failure is not fatal. It is the courage to continue that counts."[1] Explain how this maxim fits into the Christian life.

---

1   This has been widely attributed to Winston Churchill, but apparently he is not the one who said it.

Reflection Questions

01 As part of today's reflection, consider the last time you gave in to sexual temptation and answer the following questions.

    A Did you put up a good fight in the face of temptation? If so, how?

    B What eventually led you to give in?

    C Did you experience negative thoughts after your failure?

    D Did you respond biblically to those thoughts, or did you wallow in them?

02 Whether you are facing temptation or reacting to a failure, if you're going to experience lasting victory, you cannot just allow temptation or failure to keep you down! Take some time to identify where you fail to fight (either before or after a fall), and express a new commitment to change in those areas.

Day Complete ✓

THE UNEXPECTED RESCUE

Jim's Testimony (Graduated 2004)

Gaining victory over masturbation, and the lustful fantasies that went with it, was not easy. And it didn't happen instantly.

I was introduced to masturbation by an older relative around age 11. The intense pleasure immediately captivated me and quickly escalated into a daily habit. Later it would become multiple times a day and require an active life of finding images and creating fantasies to fuel my lustful habit. Many times I made a "commitment" to stop, but any degree of victory was always short-lived.

By the time I arrived at Pure Life Ministries I was desperate. I wanted sexual sin out of my life completely. But I had given over to masturbation and saturated

my mind in sexual fantasy for so long that this stronghold of sexual sin would not topple easily. Most days were full of intense battles. Failures led to despair and ushered in the lie of the enemy: "You haven't changed at all." This played into the feeling I had that I wasn't a fighter, the kind of guy it took to battle through for victory. And the thought that I might have to fight these temptations for the rest of my life was overwhelming.

One day, a staff member at Pure Life gave a little teaching on how we are *always* fighting. We are either battling against the corrupt desires of our flesh, or we are fighting against God. As he spoke, I realized I had spent years opposing

God and His commands in order to satiate my sinful desires. And one thing I could strongly affirm is that "the way of transgressors is hard." (Proverbs 13:15 KJV) My whole life had been a battle—but it had been a battle against God. This truth gave me the inspiration to turn and begin fighting my corrupt desires.

Even when the battles were intense, I knew I dare not give up. God's Word promised victory in Jesus, and I was determined to experience that victory. Instead of despair, failures led me to the Cross, and each time I encountered the Lord there I received a fresh infusion of His power for my battle.

As I continued to feed on God's Word and cry out to Him, days of victory turned into weeks of victory. I memorized the Sermon on the Mount because I saw so much of the Lord's heart revealed in it. I practiced reciting it different ways, trying to imagine how it sounded when Jesus originally spoke the words. I made a point of reciting it to myself every night as I lay in bed drifting off to sleep. And I discovered that the pornographic imagery and fantasies couldn't gain a foothold while I was reciting Scripture. Sometimes I found myself wakening in the middle of the night, and I was still quoting Scripture in my mind. The Lord was occupying my thoughts and guarding me even while I was asleep!

Of course there are still battles to be fought, but I've fallen in love with Jesus, my Lord and Savior. He has won my heart! And He has fulfilled His promise to establish victory over sexual sin in my life.

A Study in God's Word

Habitual sexual sin is a pit of darkness which we have dug with our own two hands. The further into sin one goes and the longer he remains in it, the deeper that pit becomes. Coming out of a pit of sin such as this does not come without a battle—and *only in the realm of wishful idealism does one win every battle he encounters.* However, for the person who sincerely wants to be free, desires to walk in obedience to the Lord and longs to be near Him, victory may just come when he least expects it.

✍ Look up Psalm 18:6 (which is written in past tense) and write it out as a present tense prayer to the Lord.

Psalm 107 is an amazing account of four different people groups, each of which found their way out of their difficult situations. Here are those groups:

+ Those who wandered in the wilderness (vv. 4-9)
+ Those who sat in prisons of darkness (vv. 10-16)
+ Those who were "fools" (vv. 17-22)
+ Those who went out to sea (vv. 23-32)

In Scripture, the wilderness was considered the haunt of demons (Matthew 4:1); darkness was Satan's domain (Colossians 1:13); "fools" were in bondage to sin (Proverbs 26:11); the "sea" represented the place of serpents and dragons (Isaiah 27:1). In other words, all the people involved had put themselves into the position of being controlled by the enemy.

01   With all of that in mind, compare these four people groups with each other and write a paragraph that explains the following:

A   What these people had done to get themselves into trouble;
B   How the Lord may have used the situation to ultimately benefit the people;
C   How the Lord rescued the people;
D   What the outcome was for the people.

02 Read Psalm 107:1 and 43 which describe the mercy (Hebrew, *hhesed*) of the Lord. *Hhesed* ("mercy" NKJV, "lovingkindness" NASB, "love" NIV, "steadfast love" ESV) is actually a very important term in the OT. It describes God's passionate desire to meet the needs of people. Meditate on these two verses and then describe God's desire relating to your struggles with pornography.

Reflection Questions

01 What do you think the people in Psalm 107 were thinking and feeling right before God answered their cries? What do you think they felt when God rescued them from their distress?

02 If you were in these people's shoes, would you have expected God to meet you with mercy right where you were? Or would you have thought that you were going to have to look somewhere else for deliverance?

The incredible truth about God's grace is that He can use even our failures for our good. However, this does not negate the fact that sin can often have severe consequences. For instance, God instantly forgave King David of his sin when he repented, but he paid a severe price: his newborn son died, his family was torn apart by infighting, and his own son even tried to steal the kingdom from him.

03   Why do you think God allows sin to have serious consequences? What has your attitude been when you've had to face the consequences of your own sin?

04   Compare Psalm 107:12 to Matthew 11:28-30. Have you ever considered that God has been trying to use the negative consequences of your sin to draw you closer to Himself and to give you the inward rest He provides? Write out your thoughts.

🕊 **Prayer Point**
Does what you've learned today change your perspective on His heart toward you in those specific situations? If you're still struggling to see His goodness and mercy, spend some time asking Him to make these truths real to you.

Day Complete ✓

Day Thirty-Seven

SAVING FAITH

Watch Truth #19:
*Faith is the Victory Over
Sexual Addiction*

Mason's Story (Graduated 2017)

I have always had the tendency to live by my feelings. By the time I was a teenager, I developed a habit of doing what I felt like at any given time. However, adults often put restraints on me, and it was clear that if I rebelled I would be punished, so I would comply. But when this happened, I sought revenge by pouting and making life miserable for those who prevented me from having what I wanted.

I enrolled in the Residential Program at Pure Life Ministries at the age of nineteen, having lost all real hope of gaining victory over the tyranny of my own desires. I didn't believe I could ever be free of my destructive cycles of sexual sin. This attitude came as a result of years of crushed hopes as I made attempt after futile attempt to gain victory over my sin.

Early in my time at Pure Life, I heard something that revived my hope in the possibility of change. My counselor told me that God has given me the freedom at any time to choose to obey Him as an act of my will.

Soon after he told me this, I remember waking up one morning and feeling completely dead inside. I was depressed and my mind felt numb. I was familiar with this. In the past, it had always marked the time I would give up on pursuing the Lord and turn back to pornography to help me feel good again.

That's when my counselor's words came back to me. I reasoned in my mind: *This seems crazy to me, but I'll do the same thing I've always done unless I choose to obey the Lord, even though I feel nothing.* Listlessly, I gathered my Bible and prayer journal and found a quiet place to sit. The thought suddenly came to me that I could turn the Word of God into prayers of thanks to the Lord. No one was around, so I started to read my favorite passages out loud and said, "Thank you, Lord." It felt like I was choking on each word, but kept going, "Thank you, Jesus." After some time of persevering, I noticed something unexpected happening. It was getting easier!

Before I knew it, a powerful sense of the presence of God enveloped me. I was caught up in worshiping the Lord and tears of gratitude started welling up in my eyes. My emotions had completely been transformed by a simple act of persistent obedience.

From this experience I learned that there was a deeper dimension of God that was accessible to me when I chose to act in obedience rather than my own feelings. I realized that I could apply this truth to many other areas of my life. I learned to practice simple obedience when the desire to lust came upon me or when the pangs of withdrawal from pornography suddenly hit. Armed with this faith, I soon began to win battles I had never been able to win before! Obedience in this simple area enabled me to gain freedom from pornography and masturbation.

A Study in God's Word

Hebrews 11:1 has been coined Scripture's definition of faith. Well, it might be a partial definition, but it certainly isn't a comprehensive definition. It's like trying to define "American life" with one sentence. How could you? To really make a person from one of the world's less-advanced, impoverished nations understand what it's like to be an American, you would have to tell them all kinds of stories, describe various aspects of what it is like to live here and so on. Likewise, the Lord had to provide mankind with the entire Bible—66 different books—to make people understand the reality of faith.

01   2 Corinthians 5:7 says, "We live by faith, not by sight." (NIV) Consider the difference between "sight" and "faith." Offer some concrete examples of what faith should look like in a person's life.

A

B

C

02 Explain in your own words the purpose behind the process referred to in James 1:2-3.

03 Read James 2:14-26 which describes how a person's behavior reveals the reality of his or her faith. Keep in mind that the "works" James is referring to are not the performance of the religious ceremonies the Pharisees and Judaisers relied upon to save themselves. The "works" he's talking about would be much more in line with the kinds of activities and attitudes present in the lives of true believers. Give a list of ten types of Christian behavior that would reflect a sincere life of faith.

A   F

B   G

C   H

D   I

E   J

Reflection Questions

Over the past four decades, thousands of professing Christian men have come through the Pure Life Ministries counseling programs. In our experience, there are two main possibilities to explain why any individual may not yet have experienced freedom from his sexual addiction. First, many of these men have grown up in church, but have never truly come to the place where they have entered into *the faith*. Second, some of these men have failed to learn how to walk in the vibrant spiritual life that is accessed *by faith*.

As a biblical counselor, it can be difficult to discern which of the two groups a man may belong to. Here, we'll give you the benefit of the doubt and assume that you are in the second group of people. So the following questions will be geared toward helping you learn how to walk in the spiritual power that comes by faith in Jesus Christ.

01 In Mason's story at the beginning of today's study, he shared how he could not find victory over sexual sin until he stopped living by his feelings. Has this been the pattern of your life as well? How has living by your feelings made it easier for you to give over to sexual sin?

02 In the video accompanying today's study you heard the statement, "The bigger God is in our thinking, the smaller our problems seem in comparison." What kind of thoughts typically occupy your mind? How would thinking about God lead you into the reality of a victorious life in God?

As you've seen already, our natural thinking and feelings are often enemies that hinder us from truly walking in victory, and in order to walk by faith, we must trust in God's Word more than we trust how we think or feel. (see Romans 15:4,13)

03 Write down at least three Scriptures you have been clinging to in your fight for true freedom. If you haven't been using Scripture in your fight for faith, now would be a good time to find some promises to hold onto in your daily battles for freedom.

✍ Scripture One

✍ Scripture Two

✍ Scripture Three

Day Complete ✓

Day Thirty-Eight

BELIEVING FOR VICTORY

Eric's Story (Graduated 2017)

"God, if you don't do something, I am not going to make it!"

That was my cry as I stood in the driveway outside of my house, fed up with my continual falls into sexual sin. I had been trying for two years to get free from my addiction to sexual sin. In my mind, I had tried everything in my power to get free, but my track record remained the same: defeat after defeat after defeat. I could not win this battle. I was headed for a lifetime of sin and a path straight to hell unless God stepped in to save me. So, I cried out to Him.

Now, I'd love to tell you that the moment I made this plea for help, the Lord's presence suddenly filled me with the needed faith to gain the victory! But, no, it was not that easy. It took time. It took faith. And faith was something that I had very little of at that point. What I did have was a desperation to be free.

For the next month-and-a-half, I went through the toughest spiritual battle I had ever faced. Each morning I would attempt to spend time with the Lord but then would get hit with attack after attack from the enemy of my soul. It seemed like his barrage of accusations and doubts would pound me over and over until I just gave up. The worst part of it was how completely helpless I felt against his attacks. My faith was so miniscule, so weak that I felt like I had nothing with which to defend myself.

As I continued to do my best to press on, I began to notice that help was actually coming from Heaven. It seemed that out of nowhere the Lord would swoop in with some truth from His Word that I could stand on. This would not only dispel the lies of the enemy but would also lodge something inside of me that strengthened my resolve to keep going.

For ninety days this battle raged: the enemy would come in with his lies, and then the Lord would come in with His truth. But at the end of that time, I found that the Lord had gained ground inside me and my faith had been greatly strengthened. This faith was so substantial that it has now stood the test of time over a period of nearly ten years.

Looking back, if it had not been for God's promises and the truths in His Word, I would still be living a defeated life. His words were all I had to cling to, and cling to them I did. Through it all, I now have a testimony that the God who made those promises is faithful to fulfill them.

A Study in God's Word

David once wrote, "This I know, that God is for me. In God, whose word I praise, in the Lord, whose word I praise, in God I trust; I shall not be afraid." (Psalm 56:9b-11a, ESV) He apparently wrote this right after the Lord rescued him from the Philistines as seen in 1 Samuel 21. David was in his early twenties when he experienced this deliverance. How did he gain such confidence in God at such a young age?

Undoubtedly his confidence began out in the wilderness tending his flock of sheep. It was there that he came to know the Lord. The utter solitude of the desert and the fears of being alone in the midst of wild animals must have driven him to his knees. Let's take a look at a handful of dangers David had faced by this time in his life.

01   Read 1 Samuel 17:34-35 and tell the story in your own words about what this young teenager had to face out there in the wilderness.

04   Let's go back to what David said in Psalm 56: "This I know, that God is for me." Let's reinforce that a little bit. Read 1 Timothy 2:4. The Greek word most Bibles translate as "desires" is *thelo*, which is often used to describe the will of God. Rewrite this verse in your own words using "the will of God" and personalizing it to yourself.

05   Of course, it goes without saying that people must repent. Read 2 Peter 3:9 in light of everything you have studied today and explain what you have learned.

Reflection Questions

01   In the past, have you ever felt confident to face the difficulties of life or overcome some behavior because of some quality you had (intelligence, will-power, knowledge, prior experience)? How might putting your trust in those things have undermined your confidence in God's power?

02 As you fight to overcome sexual sin, what would it look like for you to put all of your confidence in God?

03 As you approach the end of this study, are you coming to the firm conviction that true freedom is possible? Explain why or why not.

04 By now you've surely realized that faith can be a real battle. Satan will do everything to attack your faith, because faith is the victory that overcomes his dark kingdom! Below is a list of short prayers that you can use to plead with God for greater faith. Pick the ones that resonate with you the most and write them on a note card as a reminder when in prayer.

- Lord, please send an alarm into my spirit that will shake me out of any wretched complacency and spur me into holy action.
- Lord, I need a great deepening of my faith—help me overcome any cynical attitudes that lead me to trust in myself.
- Lord, I don't want to be double-minded, full of wavering doubts. Infuse my heart with rock-solid faith.
- Cement into me a conviction about spiritual matters. Make me a man (or woman) of certainty about what is pleasing to You. Give me the power of a made-up mind.
- My plea, Lord, is that when You return You will find faith in my heart, certainty in my beliefs and conviction in my life.
- Make me a man (or woman) of the Truth who can discern the lies of the enemy. Help me, Lord, to shut out the voice of the world with all its intoxicating lies. Help me to live in the Truth and to have faith in the Truth.

🕊 **Prayer Point**
Conclude today's study with a prayer of faith and commitment. Express your belief and hope in the Lord, and proclaim your confidence that God is going to bring you through to victory as you rely on His strength, wage war against your sin and continue to fight the good fight of faith.

Day Complete ✓

Day Thirty-Nine

SOWING INTO YOUR FUTURE

Watch Truth #20:
*A Lifestyle of Obedience is a
Lifestyle of Blessing*

Lucas' Story (Graduated 2021)

When I was a young boy, I had no idea how far my disobedience would carry me away from the Lord. What began as small indulgences of curiosity rapidly turned into a lifestyle of seeking as much pleasure and comfort as I could find.

By the end of high school, my eyes were fixed on what the world could offer me and I saw the things of God as a hindrance to true fulfillment. The more I gave myself over to what God had forbidden the more I wanted it. I was becoming what the apostle Paul calls an "inventor of evil." (Romans 1:30) My immersion in the world of fantasy and pornography was not only destroying my faith in God, but it was actually causing me to hate Him. Nevertheless, the Lord would regularly convict me about my sin in an attempt to lead me to repentance. These acts of kindness only caused me to harden my heart and despise Him even more. I got to the point where I was actually cursing Him and telling Him to leave me alone.

In His longsuffering nature, God allowed my sinful lifestyle to take its course, knowing that I would eventually cry out to Him for mercy. He certainly answered that cry and has led me out of the darkness I once lived in. He has taught me through this process how to reverse the direction of my life by sowing to the Spirit.

Over a decade of worldly living is being undone by incorporating the disciplines of daily time spent with God in His Word and in prayer. He has opened my eyes to the dangers of dwelling on ungodly thinking through fantasy, criticism or even grumbling. Instead, I have learned to fight against my natural inclinations and seek ways to please Him. Rather than living in constant lust, He has taught me to be attentive to the needs of others.

The discontentment and complaining spirit that once ruled my inner life is being changed by developing a grateful heart. I did not find freedom through a one-time prayer for deliverance. It came through abiding in Christ. As I have endeavored to sow to the Spirit, I've been filled with joy and my desire to abide in Him has only increased. He has surely turned my life around and made it a true blessing!

A Study in God's Word

As you are nearing the end of this journey, it's time to start thinking about where you go from here. Hopefully the last thirty-eight days have really helped establish a walk with God that will unfold as a lifestyle of righteousness and a dismantling of your self-life. Of course, the rest of your life, not just forty days, must be one of continual growth in Christlikeness. As Solomon said, "the path of the righteous is like the light of dawn that shines brighter and brighter until full day." (Proverbs 4:18)

Every day you are clearing a path into your future by the things you do. If you are doing good things, i.e., godly behavior, you will find that it will be easier to live a righteous life the next day. On the other hand, if you are indulging in sinful behavior today, the path into wickedness will be easier to follow tomorrow.

01   Paul offers two scenarios in Galatians 6:7-8. The first part of the equation for each scenario is supplied (sowing) and, in your own words, you fill in how you think things will go in your future (reaping).

    A   If I sow to my flesh, I will…

    B   If I sow to the Spirit, I will…

02 Read the following verses which show various comparisons between righteous and unrighteous behavior. Explain in your own words the difference in outcomes you see for each behavior.

📖 **Psalm 1:6**

Righteous	Unrighteous

📖 **Proverbs 10:29**

Righteous	Unrighteous

📖 **Proverbs 12:15**

Righteous	Unrighteous

📖 **Proverbs 15:9**

Righteous	Unrighteous

02 Read 1 Samuel 17:36-37 and describe the confidence David expressed.

03 Now read 1 Samuel 17:40-53. The story of David and Goliath is known around the world. It is typically used to illustrate a weak person (or company, or nation, etc.) going up against someone more powerful. Of course, the main point of it is missed by most people. The point wasn't that a weaker person found a way to beat a stronger opponent. The point was that David won the battle because he trusted God to defend His name and His people. Can you see how, despite Goliath's advantage in size, armor and weaponry, David went into that battle in total confidence because of his deep trust in God? This is the very kind of certainty about God's good intentions you need for the battle you are engaged in. Briefly discuss how this account in Scripture helps you in your current battles.

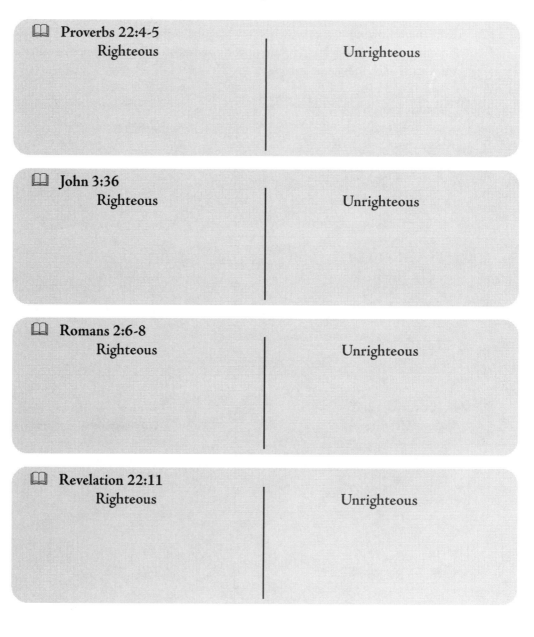

Proverbs 22:4-5

Righteous   Unrighteous

John 3:36

Righteous   Unrighteous

Romans 2:6-8

Righteous   Unrighteous

Revelation 22:11

Righteous   Unrighteous

Reflection Questions

01   Can you see how the choices we've made in the past shape the life we live in the present?

02   Now think about your future. God has laid out two paths before you: blessing or cursing; life or death; sowing to the Spirit or sowing to the flesh. Considering what you learned in Question #2 above, make a list of at least 5 blessings that will be yours if you choose to follow God by sowing to the Spirit. Then, make a list of at least 5 negative consequences that are likely to occur in your life if you choose to sow to your flesh.

Blessings	Consequences
A	A
B	B
C	C
D	D
E	E

03   The obvious choice is to choose Life that you might truly live, and enjoy a rich, deep, and satisfying relationship with the Lord and all the blessings that He has for you! Let's personalize the list of blessings you wrote down. How would those blessings manifest in your own life? For example: If you wrote down that sowing to the Spirit would give you more peace, think about an area in your life where an increase of peace would change your situation.

Day Complete ✓

Day Forty

GOD'S BLESSINGS

Sebastian's Story (Graduated 2022)

In many ways, I was a typical American Christian a few years ago. I had been married for twenty-one years and had three adult children. My wife and I both worked fulltime jobs and even had a side business as well. We had it all: a home, cars, food, and money in the bank. Yet, in spite of living the American dream, I felt very dissatisfied in my heart.

It was then that I began entertaining cravings in my heart that I had suppressed over the years. It was the desire to become involved in homosexuality. Those carnal desires soon overtook me and I began engaging in secret trysts with other men. Every indulgence took me deeper into the realm of darkness.

Through this entire period I continued going to church and playing the part. Each time I gave over, I would simply ask the Lord to forgive me—convinced that His grace covered it all. I even started asking Him to take away my sexual lust and could not understand when He didn't answer this prayer. Instead of humbling myself, I became angry with Him.

Eventually it all came out, and I ended up at the Pure Life Ministries Residential Program. My wife was shocked when she discovered what I had been doing and filed for divorce. I watched a lifetime of hard work fall apart before my eyes. The stripping down I went through left me feeling lonely, poor, lost and broken.

I began to cry out to God and repent of who I was. The more heart-felt repenting I did, the more I began to see the Lord for who He was. His love became the true blessing of my life. I knew that I deserved hell, yet He lavished me with love, compassion, patience and mercy.

There was a time when the only praying I did was to ask God for His blessings. Now, having lost nearly every possession I owned and every meaningful relationship I had, I found myself uninterested in looking for outward blessings because He had become so important to me.

He has truly become all I ever needed. I seek Him in the morning, throughout my day, and before I go to bed. Although I do miss my wife and kids tremendously, He is enough to satisfy my deepest longings. He has become my prize, my gift, the love of my life, my best friend. He is mine now and for all eternity.

A Study in God's Word

One could not possibly overstate the goodness of God's character. He loves His people and it is in His heart to bless them. In fact, the only reason He doesn't lavish them with more blessings is because He knows that it would harm them; e.g., the tragic life of Solomon.

Time and again we've heard the testimony from those who complete the Pure Life program: "God has been so good to me. He's blessed me beyond anything I ever imagined possible!" Restored marriages, renewed relationships with children, the perfect job opportunities, open doors for ministry, international travels, miraculous protection, divine connections of one sort or another, every need perfectly supplied—and on and on the list goes. Even in the face of life's challenges and difficulties, their cup of blessing continues to overflow and give testimony to God's goodness. And yet these same men are quick to insist that their greatest blessing has been their relationship with the Lord. Whatever else He has done for them, having a rich, vibrant life in God is the true blessing.

✍ Write out Psalm 34:8 in your own words.

The goodness of God is seen in a myriad of ways. It is one of His most beautiful qualities. When Moses asked to see God's glory, the Lord responded by saying that He would make "all His goodness" pass by him.

01 Look up the following verses regarding God's goodness and briefly describe what you learn.

📖 Psalm 23:6

📖 Psalm 86:5

📖 Psalm 25:8

📖 Psalm 125:4

📖 Psalm 84:11

📖 Lamentations 3:25

02 Because God is good, He loves to bless those who obey Him. Read the following psalms regarding His blessings, focusing on the type of person described as "blessed" in these verses. Also consider what ways He chooses to bless these people. Briefly describe what you learn.

📖 Psalm 1:1

📖 Psalm 84:5

📖 Psalm 32:1-2

📖 Psalm 94:12

📖 Psalm 40:4

📖 Psalm 106:3

📖 Psalm 41:1

📖 Psalm 119:1-2

📖 Psalm 128:1-2

Reflection Questions

If you've begun to incorporate the truths from this study journal, then your life has definitely begun to turn around. That should be a tremendous encouragement to you. Just remember this: The new life you're experiencing is a direct result of how you've applied God's Word to your life. If you continue to practice what you've learned, your path will only grow brighter and brighter.

01 What is the most impactful thing you've learned about yourself during this study?

02 What is the most impactful thing you've learned about the Lord during this study?

03   What is the most significant way your spiritual life has improved during this study?

04   How have the truths you've learned helped you with your porn addiction?

05   What habits have you established that you need to continue to maintain even after the study is over?

🕊 **Prayer Point**

And lastly, take some time to pray. Thank the Lord for what He's already done in your life. Ask Him to help you continue to implement what you have learned through this video series. And express confidence in what He has in store for you in the future.

Day Complete ✓

☑ FINAL CHECK-IN

As we're wrapping up this study, I would like to add my voice to the other 40 brothers who have testified in this journal. You've already seen the first video, where I shared my basic testimony of getting free from habitual sexual sin. For this final check-in, I would like to take you back to the painful experience I had in 1991 that I shared in the twelfth video, *Repentance Must Become an Integral Part of a New Lifestyle*.

At that point, Pure Life Ministries was five years old. As I shared in the video, Kathy and I had visited a small church located nearby to decide if we wanted to bring the men in the residential program there on Sundays.

The pastor preached from Luke 6 that morning about living out the love of God to other people. As he concluded his sermon, he invited those who felt they needed to get right with God to come forward to the altar. I can't say I was stirred emotionally, because I wasn't. Nevertheless, I did feel convicted about my lack of love and knew that the Lord was tugging on my heart, so I dutifully responded to the pastor's invitation.

I was as surprised as anyone when the Lord met me at that altar and gave me a sight of how prideful and self-centered I was. The revelation of my lack of love for others provoked tears, which all too quickly became a torrent of deep, sobbing grief.

I have to say that bawling like a baby in front of that entire congregation was a humiliating experience. But even the embarrassment I experienced was part of God's plan for me that morning. You see, in His world, His actions sometimes seem to utterly contradict our thinking. The Lord was doing a deep work inside me that would prove to be a defining moment of my life. I became a little bit different that day: less full of myself and more like Christ.

Why am I sharing this story with you? I wanted to give you a snapshot into the life of a man *six years after* being set free from sexual sin. In other words, getting my life turned around was only the beginning.

You too are on a journey, and during this long trek through life, you are going to have many experiences that the Lord is going to use for the purpose of molding you into the image of His Son. (Romans 8:29)

My hope and prayer is that He has been able to use this study journal to help you get headed in the right direction. You will have your ups and downs, successes and failures. The important thing to remember is that you must keep fighting, keep pressing on and doing your utmost to obey the Lord. As you do this, you will find that His grace will cover you and empower you to finish your race well.

I'll end this testimony with these inspiring words from our Lord's brother:

> *Now to him who is able to keep you from stumbling and to present you blameless before the presence of His glory with great joy, to the only God, our Savior, through Jesus Christ our Lord, be glory, majesty, dominion, and authority, before all time and now and forever. Amen.*
> **Jude 1:24-25 (ESV)**

Okay, now let's look at the commitments you should have implemented from the Check-Ins on Day 10, Day 20 and Day 30.

- ✓ I have been doing this study every day.
- ✓ I have cut off all avenues to pornography.
- ✓ I have told my spiritual leader about my secret life.
- ✓ I have established a consistent prayer life.
- ✓ I have started a gratitude journal.
- ✓ I have implemented my plan to have regular fellowship with my wife or other believers.
- ✓ I will not watch any ungodly entertainment.
- ✓ I will eliminate easy access to any social media accounts that have been a consistent avenue of failure.
- ✓ I will make plans to continue my daily Bible time after this study ends.

Now, let's add some final commitments.

☐ **If I am married, I will confess my sexual sin to my wife.**

For those of you who are married, God's intention is that your wife be your closest companion, helper and confidante. But this cannot happen if you have secrets! If you haven't already confessed to her what you've been doing in secret, it's time to make things right. Consider the following suggestions regarding making this confession.

1 **Plan a specific time for your confession.** Bringing this up when your wife is busy, or stressed, or preoccupied with the kids will be counterproductive. Plan for a time when you can have an uninterrupted conversation.

2 **Pray about your confession.** You need to come to her in a contrite spirit. Pray that your confession would contain no minimizing, justifying or blameshifting. Pray that you would have the grace to accept whatever reaction you receive from your wife with true humility. Ask God to uphold her when she receives this distressing news.

3 **Make a full confession.** As painful as it will be for your wife to hear what you have done, it will be much harder if you make a series of partial confessions. You must bring everything to the light at once.

4 **Leave graphic detail out of your confession.** The last thing your wife needs are all of the details about your sexual sin. Too much detail tends to plague a woman's mind for days, months, or even years. A true confession must contain the scope and extent of what you've done (*I've been watching pornography _____ times a week for _____ years*), but not overly graphic (*I like _____ type of women*). If you'd like further help in preparing for this confession, we've filmed a video that contains much more wisdom about handling this situation. It can be viewed by scanning the QR code to the left.

☐ **I will limit the amount of time I am spending on social media and entertainment.**

Earlier in this study you saw that a key ingredient to finding freedom from pornography is to take a stand against *all* ungodly entertainment. Now it's time to take things a step further. You must not only be cautious about the kinds of content you consume, but *how much*. Even the most innocuous content will have a negative effect on your spiritual life if you spend too much time in it. Prayerfully come up with a reasonable game plan as to how you will handle this; make sure you include clear-cut limitations that you will abide by. It's also a good idea to share these limitations with someone who will assist in keeping you accountable.

☐ **I will prayerfully consider what way God could use me to meet the needs of others.**

Did you know that God gives each of us specific desires and abilities that He can use to meet the needs of other people? Some believers are gifted with the ability to meet physical needs, others with the resources to meet material needs, still others with the ability to empathize with hurting people, and so on. Now that you have allowed the Lord to break the hold of your addiction to pornography, it's time to begin making yourself available to the Lord so that He can use your life and giftings to help other people. Make this a matter of prayer. (If you'd like help discerning your spiritual gift, there is a booklet called "Understanding Spiritual Gifts" available through the Institute in Basic Life Principles that may be of help to you).

Endnotes

Day Three

i   C.S. Lewis, *The Quotable Lewis* (Wheaton, IL: Tyndale House Publishers, 1989) p. 151.

ii *Inspiring Quotations Contemporary and Classical* (Nashville, TN: Thomas Nelson Publishers, 1988) p. 177.

iii Steve Gallagher, *Intoxicated with Babylon* (Dry Ridge, KY: Pure Life Ministries, 2019) p. 15.

Day Four

i   Steve Gallagher, *Walking in Truth in a World of Lies* (Dry Ridge, KY: Pure Life Ministries, 2020) p. 191.

Day Six

i   John MacArthur, "Fundamentals—Self-Discipline-Part One," accessed at www.gty/library/sermons-library.com.

Day Eleven

i   www.dictionary.com/browse/hedonism.

Day Twelve

i   https://en.wikipedia.org>wiki>experiment.

Day Twenty-Four

i   Paul Gardner, *Exegetical Commentary on the New Testament* (Grand Rapids, MI: Zondervan Publishers, 2018).

Stay connected with Pure Life Ministries!

Smartphone App

In our sexualized culture, it's nearly impossible to avoid sensual imagery when browsing the internet. With our smartphone app, you can have access to content that will encourage you to pursue holiness and purity of heart and life, even if your phone is completely locked down. You'll be able to view:

- Powerful sermons
- More of our mini video series like "20 Truths that Helped Me in My Battle with Porn Addiction"
- Compelling testimonies, blog articles and our weekly podcast

The app is completely free and available for both Android and iOS devices.

The Pure Life Ministries Podcast

Our weekly podcast will take you where real life meets real Christianity as we tackle the tough issues for those struggling with sexual sin. In a world teeming with conflicting opinions, this show looks to God and His Word alone as we diagnose the key issues and seek to prescribe the cure. Listen to individual episodes at purelifeministries.org/podcast or subscribe wherever you get your podcasts.

The Narrow Way eNewsletter

Get solid, biblical content from Pure Life Ministries delivered right to your inbox! Designed to help you live a pure and holy life before God, this monthly eNewsletter features articles, podcasts, videos and more. To sign up, just visit **purelifeministries.org/enews**

Explore our Counseling Programs

Residential Care

The most intense and involved counseling Pure Life offers comes through the **Residential Program** (9 months), in Dry Ridge, Kentucky. The godly and sober atmosphere on our 45-acre campus provokes the hunger for God and deep repentance that destroys the hold of sin in men's lives.

Help At Home

In addition to our Residential Program, we also offer the **Overcomers At-Home Program** (for men) and **Create in Me a Pure Heart Program** (for women). These 16-week programs bring the same life-changing truths and counseling to men and women right where they are.

Care for Wives

Pure Life Ministries also offers help to wives of men in sexual sin through our 12-week **At-Home Program for Wives**. Our wives' counselors have suffered through the trials and storms of such a discovery and can offer a devastated wife a sympathetic ear and the biblical solutions that worked in their lives.

For more information about these and other resources visit:

www.purelifeministries.org

or call: 859-824-4444

OTHER RESOURCES AVAILABLE
BY PURE LIFE MINISTRIES

At the Altar of Sexual Idolatry
At the Altar of Sexual Idolatry DVD Curriculum
At the Altar of Sexual Idolatry Workbook
A Biblical Guide to Counseling the Sexual Addict
Create in Me a Pure Heart
Create in Me a Pure Heart Workbook
From Ashes to Beauty
He Leads Me Beside Still Waters
i: the root of sin exposed
Intoxicated with Babylon
A Lamp Unto My Feet
Living in Victory
Out of the Depths of Sexual Sin
Pressing on Toward the Heavenly Calling
Standing Firm through the Great Apostasy
The Time of Your Life in Light of Eternity
The Walk of Repentance
Walking in Truth in a World of Lies
When His Secret Sin Breaks Your Heart
The Word of Their Testimony